CULTURAL MELANCHOLY

CULTURAL MELANCHOLY

READINGS OF RACE, IMPOSSIBLE MOURNING, AND AFRICAN AMERICAN RITUAL

JERMAINE SINGLETON

UNIVERSITY OF ILLINOIS PRESS
URBANA, CHICAGO, AND SPRINGFIELD

Library of Congress Cataloging-in-Publication Data
Singleton, Jermaine, 1974–
Cultural melancholy : readings of race, impossible
mourning, and African American ritual /
Jermaine Singleton.
pages cm
Includes bibliographical references and index.
ISBN 978-0-252-03962-1 (hardback) —
ISBN 978-0-252-09771-3 (e-book)
1. American literature—African American
authors—History and criticism. 2. Grief in literature.
3. Mourning customs—United States. 4. African
Americans—Race identity—History. I. Title.
PS153.N5S553   2015
810.9'896073—dc23   2015019415

For Margaret and James Singleton (my loving parents)

CONTENTS

ACKNOWLEDGMENTS

This book has several midwives. First, I would like to thank my editors at the University of Illinois Press, Dawn Durante and Larin McLaughlin, for believing in the promise of my original manuscript and shepherding it through a lengthy yet rewarding review process. I appreciate their thoughtful and helpful comments and their work in finding the remarkable readers this manuscript needed to help me achieve my original goals for it.

At Hamline University, Fernando Delgado and John Matachek, who served consecutively in the Dean's Office of the College of Liberal Arts and Sciences, provided much material support for this project. I am grateful for the editorial support of Erin Derwin and Geof Garvey. The moral support of Kris Deffenbacher, Marcela Kostihova, Mike Reynolds, Deanna Thompson, Susie Steinbach, Nancy Holland, Duane Cady, Jenny Kiel, Andrea Bell, Jean Strait, and Earl Schwartz has made Hamline a true professional home. I am grateful to Alice Moorhead, Veena Deo, and Mark Olson for encouraging me to approach teaching in an experimental fashion and being such remarkable mentors over the years. Most of all, I thank my students. This book could not exist without the undergraduate students who enrolled in "American Melancholy," "Reading Whiteness," "Reading Masculinities," and "Dramas of Race" over the years at Hamline University. I'm a lucky bloke to have had students who open their minds willingly to insurgent critical thinking and practice. Reading the underside of American history by interrogating "the obvious and well-received" with you all has been most rewarding.

I'm deeply indebted to my intellectual and professional mentors from my days at the University of Minnesota—John S. Wright, John Mowitt, Timothy

Brennan, Jani Scandura, Roderick A. Ferguson, and Tom Augst—who saw and invested in my potential. Michelle Wright's support made an important difference in this project's completion; for your generosity of time and spirit, good advice, and strategic collegiality during a time when I needed it most, I am very grateful. For sharpening my critical inquiry and practice skills, I thank the panel chairs and audiences at the American Men's Studies Association, the Tenth International New Directions in the Humanities Conference; the Midwest Modern Languages Association; the Northeast Modern Languages Association; the Melancholic States Conference; the Association for the Psychoanalysis of Culture and Society; the Working Through Psychoanalysis Conference; the Space, Place, and Memory Symposium; the Universities of Michigan and Minnesota; and Leeds and Lancaster Universities. I also thank the staff of the Beinecke Rare Books and Manuscript Library at Yale University and the Schomberg Center for Research in Black Culture. For reading all or parts of my manuscript, I thank Gwen Bergner, Brenda Helt, Michelle Wright, Karla Holloway, Carol E. Henderson, Harry J. Elam Jr., Mike Reynolds, Tobias Spears, Millicent Flowers, Cesar Garcia, Gena Miller, Signe Harriday, Teniece Harris, Carlos D. Sneed, Meosha Muhammad, and the anonymous readers at the University of Illinois Press. Their generosity of time, critical inquiry, and intellectual curiosity pushed this book along a steep growth curve.

The editors of *College Literature* and *MAWA Review* gave permission to reprint in revised form material that I previously published. Material from Chapter 2 first appeared in *College Literature* as "Some Losses Remain with Us: Impossible Mourning and the Prevalence of Ritual in August Wilson's *The Piano Lesson*," 36.2 (Spring 2009): 40–57. Material from Chapter 3 first appeared in *MAWA Review* as "Sacred and Silent (Man)ufacturing: Melancholy, Raced and the Gendered Politics of Testifying in James Baldwin's *Go Tell It on the Mountain*," 19.1 (June 2004): 39–57. My deep appreciation also goes to Burney J. Hollis, Kostas Mysiades, and the members of the editorial boards for *College Literature* and *MAWA Review*.

I want to thank my foot soldiers—Brenda Helt, Torino K. Fitzgerald, James E. Hill, Ivan Brown, Brendan Kramp, Ahavaha Pyrtel, Teniece Harris, and Shawn O. Thompson—who helped me discard the load of history at the intersection of racial and sexual difference so I could thrive without distraction. All of you are true friends; the personal advice and quality time over the years has been crucial to the completion of this project. I had the good fortune of meeting Marcus Mays, Davina Baldwin, Cassie Rood, Cherries Turner, Jasond Thomas, and Julio Torres during the final years of writing this book; their affection and remarkable friendship kept me awake and grounded as I finished it. For this, my friends, I will be forever grateful. Big thanks to my siblings Meosha Muhammad and James Singleton Jr. for the clarity of existence and unconditional love.

I dedicate this book to my parents, Margaret and James Singleton Sr., whose love and support equipped me to rise to the occasion with my best. I am forever grateful to have come into life through them both.

INTRODUCTION

For a moment nobody's talking, but every face looks
darkening, like the sky outside. . . . Everyone is looking at
something a child can't see. For a minute they've forgotten
the children. Maybe a kid is lying on the rug, half asleep.
. . . The silence, the darkness coming, the darkness in the
faces frightens the child obscurely. He hopes that the hand
which strokes his forehead will never stop—will never die.
He hopes that there will never come a time when the old
folks won't be sitting around the living room, talking about
where they've come from and what they've seen, and what's
happened to them and their kinfolk. . . . But something
deep and watchful in the child knows that this is bound to
end, is already ending. In a moment someone will get up
and turn on the light. Then the old folks will remember the
children and they won't talk any more that day. And when
the light fills the room, the child is filled with darkness. He
knows that every time this happens he's moved just a little
closer to that darkness outside. The darkness outside is
what the old folks have been talking about. It's what they've
come from. It's what they endure. The child knows that they
won't talk anymore because if he knows too much about
what's happened to *them*, he'll know too much too soon,
and what's going to happen to *him*.
—Baldwin, "Sonny's Blues" 1734–35

The darkness: what the old folks have come from and endured yet confiscates
the psychic life of the children well before they endure the same circumstances. The unnamed narrator of James Baldwin's "Sonny's Blues" attempts
to explain the cryptic process through which the subject-formation carries
the secrets left over from the lives of others: "As the singing filled the air the
watching, listening faces underwent a change, the eyes focusing on something
within; the music seemed to soothe a poison out of them; and time seemed,
nearly, to fall away from the sullen, belligerent, battered faces, as though they

were fleeing back to their first condition, while dreaming of their last" (1743). Such is the ubiquity of hidden affect that defies conscious recognition. Such is the psychical communion secured because and in spite of modern American nationhood's culture of racial subjugation. David L. Eng and David Kasanjian, the editors of *Loss: The Politics of Mourning*, devoted the entire anthology to the exploration of the "numerous material practices by which loss is melancholically materialized in the social and cultural realms and in the political and the aesthetic domains" (5). In *Immigrant Acts*, Lisa Lowe summarizes the phenomenon succinctly: "Culture is the terrain through which the individual speaks as a member of the contemporary national collectivity, but culture is also a mediation of history, the site through which the past returns and is remembered, however fragmented, imperfect and disavowed."[1]

Cultural Melancholy explores the disavowed claims of the past on the present through a group of cultural productions—literature, drama, and film—focused on racialized subject-formations and cultural formations. Investigating the intersection of categories of social difference, nation making, and buried social memory, this book uncovers a host of hidden dialogues—psychic and social, personal and political, individual and collective, past and present—for the purpose of dismantling the legacy effects of historical racial subjugation and inequality. *Cultural Melancholy*'s conceptual foundation follows Baldwin's essential illustration in "Sonny's Blues," suggesting that the hidden affect and disavowed social loss that binds racialized subjects across time and social space is primarily responsible for the nation's ongoing battle with the material and impalpable remains of its history of racial slavery and subjugation it cannot claim. The narrator's statement insists that the former dynamic cannot be understood in isolation from the latter. Even more, this book insists that the two dynamics are mutually constitutive, one drawing its strength from the other discreetly.

Cultural Melancholy charts new territory in the relationship between critical race studies, psychoanalysis, and performance studies. The book brings psychoanalytic paradigms of mourning and melancholia and discussions of race and performance by W.E.B. Du Bois, Frantz Fanon, Julian Carter, Diana Taylor, and Kimberly Benton into conversation with literary work on post-Emancipation America's everyday life and ritual practice to challenge scholarship that calls for the clinical separation of ethnic studies and psychoanalysis as well as the divorce of psychoanalysis and socioeconomic history and presumes that this disengagement is central to American nationhood's continued relationship with unresolved racial grievances. This study develops a theory of "cultural melancholy" that uncovers and addresses the ideological and psychical claims of the history of slavery and ongoing racial subjugation on contemporary racialized subject-formations and dominant American culture. The book extends psychoanalytic revisions of Freudian melancholia, urging us not to lose sight of the hidden affect that works through cultural practice to reconstitute itself across time and social space as it shapes and forecloses identification possibilities.[2]

My historically, materially, and psychically contingent theory of cultural melancholy not only illuminates the unexpectedly rich connections between psychoanalysis and critical race studies by providing a grammar for understanding how melancholia travels across time and social space though the radicalized subject-formation that is simultaneously individualistic and interpersonal, but also demonstrates the ways in which a reading of race and ritual that draws on psychoanalysis to place critical race studies into conversation with the critical traditions of performance studies can be politically and culturally transformative. Writing psychoanalysis into critical race studies and critical race studies back into psychoanalysis at once, the book provides a more psychically nuanced and sensitively historicist look at racialized subjects as they were produced, maintained, and interlocked across time and social space through discourse, hidden affect, and ritual in response to the ideological pressures and material crises that shaped American modernity. To that end, the book adapts models that force racialized subjects to be caught in the bind of being "one" standing in for the "many." In considering the performative and affective consolidation of the radicalized subject-formation, the book draws on performance studies and psychoanalytic theory to advance the project of critical race studies a step further by accounting for the sociological facets of race and its ontological status at once. Broadening performance studies to take up the project of critical race studies, this study explores the role theater might play in loosening the constraints of historical racial grief on contemporary social engagement.

In his 1917 essay "Mourning and Melancholia," Sigmund Freud lays out two ways of dealing with loss. Here, Freud locates melancholia at the limits of mourning. According to Freud, "mourning" is the successful integration of loss into consciousness. In "melancholia," Freud maintains, a loss that is unmourned and barred from recognition is displaced discreetly onto the subject's ego, enacting an unconscionable loss of self. For Freud, mourning is a healthy response to loss and melancholia is an unhealthy one. Mourning is healthy because "we rest assured that after a lapse of time it will be overcome," says Freud ("Mourning and Melancholia," 240). Inversely, the melancholic suffers an unconscionable loss of self, a loss that claims yet cannot be claimed.

To put this alternatively, melancholy describes a psychic state wherein losses of self are retained and barred from conscious recognition.[3]

A reading of "Sonny's Blues" that draws on psychoanalysis would seem, then, to insist upon an analysis of the short story from the logic of melancholia, as the internal darkness of Sonny, the unnamed narrator's younger brother, is suppressed and retained through his music. Sonny's internal darkness is a by-product of the darkness that has always already infiltrated the psychic lives of African America proper. Regarding these complications, then, *Cultural Melancholy* draws on work in psychoanalytic criticism that exposes the contradictions and instability of the process of subject formation at the intersection of the forces of racialization and melancholia. Like Baldwin's short story, this body of work ultimately resists Freud's binary logic of mourning and melancholia. My project challenges Freud's contention that "melancholia ensues from a pathological disposition," and thus it follows publications such as David L. Eng and Shinhee Han's "A Dialogue on Racial Melancholia," José Esteban Muñoz's *Disidentifications*, and especially Anne Cheng's *The Melancholy of Race*, which demonstrates how normative and minority subject-formations are fragile, melancholic edifices—identities constructed and imaginatively supported through a dynamic of loss and compensation—by which losses of self are disavowed and retained.

One compelling example of this ambivalence comes from James Baldwin's "Sonny's Blues." There is a key moment in the text in which Baldwin's narrator speaks to the impossible mourning that mobilizes Sonny's blues:

> All I know about music is that not many people ever really hear it. And even then, on the rare occasions when something opens within, and the music enters, what we mainly hear, or hear corroborated, are personal, private, vanishing evocations. But the man who creates the music is hearing something else, is dealing with the roar rising from the void and imposing order on it as it hits the air. (1747)

Baldwin locates Sonny's blues as a kind of chamber of melancholic flux, a treading between acknowledging and not acknowledging one's social exclusion, laying bare and domesticating one's feelings of deficit, enacting despair and hope at once. Indeed, Sonny's blues emerges from the tension between mourning and melancholia—knowing and not knowing myriad losses of self. Sonny's blues allows him to live with the darkness by engaging it on its ambivalent terms, allowing him to temporarily resolve psychic dissonance. Sonny's ritualized oscillation between mourning and melancholia at once challenges our conventional interpretation of the Freudian model of a mutually exclusive mourning and melancholia and illuminates how certain rituals emerge from this ambivalent dynamic. The crucial point to investigate, then, is why and how this impossible mourning works through ritual practice and various regimes of power (psychosocial, sexual, and linguistic) to travel across time and social space.

In reading representations of American ritual practice—people lamenting, praying, witnessing, listening, lynching, talking, and not talking together—I examine literary and cultural representations of ritual in texts that leave direction for circumventing the past's claim on the present. Depictions and enactments of ritual and performance by F. Scott Fitzgerald, Billie Holiday, August Wilson, James Baldwin, Suzan-Lori Parks, and Tony Kushner seem generally concerned with the acute manner in which ritual practice draws on Western metaphysical dualism to bind radicalized subjects—past, present, and unborn—through psychic introjections or inheritance. Rituals are the medium through which we are hailed without being hailed, giving rise to the following questions: Why is the study of ritual through the psychoanalytic paradigm of melancholia and African American social history critical to the advancement of critical race studies and psychoanalysis at once? How might ritual serve as the very cultural sites for exhuming and resuscitating our disavowed social and national possibilities? By theorizing the modes through which sociopolitical formations (like rituals of radicalization and national belonging) are linked to psycho-political formations (like melancholia), my project aims to reform and revivify what I have called theater of cultural grieving. Indeed, my final chapter draws on theater to outline political strategies for fostering the emotional intelligence and critical awareness needed to mitigate the psychic traumas brought on by ongoing rituals of racialization and national exclusion.

The chapters that follow flesh out my theory of cultural melancholy to uniquely locate the production and mediation of normative and African American subject-formations at the intersection of various modalities of difference—living and dead, past and present, here and there, physical and spiritual, race and gender, nationality and sexuality—and disavowed social loss. As the individual chapters of this book collectively illustrate, racial, gender, and sexual identifications aren't mutually exclusive realms of experience, existing in splendid isolation from each other and the demands of capital, nor can this dynamic be understood in isolation from hidden affect, disavowed social loss, and ritual.

The method of my current research is historical, cultural materialist, and interdisciplinary. My reading of American modernity is not exhaustive and thus should not be applied universally to all segments of American cultural practice; rather, it is an analysis of the cultural melancholy that emerges from particular social, historical, economic, and psychical contexts. Focusing primarily on literary and cultural representations of national belonging, texts that depict how modern social relations are directly affected by past events and circumstances, this study investigates both the psychic and material conditions that have circumscribed racialized subject-formations and social formations over time. The analysis of literature of national belonging and reflection I pursue also aims to interrogate universalizing ways of thinking about radicalized subjectivity without losing sight of, as bell hooks warns, "the specific history and experiences" of these racialized subjects and the "unique sensibilities and culture that arise from that experience."[4] It is, after all, only through a sustained and interdisciplinary—psychological, sociological, and historical—analysis of the psychical inheritances of the nation's racial history that we can do worthy battle against racism in our contemporary multiculture.

Impossible Mourning and the Renewal of Critical Race Studies and Psychoanalysis

I remain convinced that the clinical separation of psychoanalytic insights and readings of social history as well as the disciplinary divorce of ethnic studies from psychoanalysis are germane to the persistence of "race" and racism.[5] Some scholars of African American literature and culture have doubted the usefulness of using psychoanalytic paradigms to explore black cultural productions and subject-formations.[6] In *Racial Castration,* David L. Eng notes "Detractors of psychoanalytic theory have justifiably noted that, in its insistent privileging of sexuality as the organizing principle of subjectivity and loss, psychoanalysis has had little to offer the story of race or the processes of racialization"(4–5). Eng goes on to point out that "It is indispensable to incorporate socially and historically variable factors into what hitherto has been rather a-historical and essentializing psychoanalytic formulations of the construction of subjectivity" (5). Moreover, the nation's history of discrimination by way of a compulsory dehumanization of the racialized body has made critics of African American literature and culture hesitant to consider the immaterial, unquantifiable dimensions of black subjectivity in favor of reifying the notion of a "real," living and breathing black subject. I hope it will prove indispensable to trace the hidden and social loss that has gone into the construction and maintenance of a dominant, standard white ideal and the racialized social body that makes its presence legible. The ebb and flow of hidden affect and disavowed social loss across and within these categories of social difference in the name of racial identity, I hope to show, is the very place we must go to build a multiculture that relies more on our openness to change than its own stability to survive.

Amid the skepticism around the efficacy of psychoanalytic readings of African American literature and culture, *Cultural Melancholy* explores this contested union and asks the question as follows: What does psychoanalysis, particularly theories of melancholia, hold for understanding the relationship between impossible mourning, ritual practice, and the process of racialized subject formation? If the losses of self incurred by earlier generations of African Americans are not resolved and mourned, then what remains of this melancholia? How does the melancholy of a nation work through ritual practice to take residence in its racialized subject-formations? How did African American cultural resistance efforts work through the ideological forces that shaped the American union to propel post-Emancipation African America's melancholy across time and social space? How do we account for an accruing racial melancholia, as the children of a people of racial subordination and exclusion cope with their own subjugation?

As our example from "Sonny's Blues" illustrates, culture is the terrain in which the past blends inconspicuously with the present and future. "Sonny's Blues" locates culture as melancholy's vehicle of discreet time travel. Sonny's blues mediates the ineffable pain of the social loss that circumscribes his Harlem community. And to be sure, Sonny's blues serves as a secular medium through which the racialized community binds in avowed and disavowed ways. That is, Sonny's blues not only gives veiled expression to and retains his own and the narrator's suffering, providing a melancholic strategy that connects them uniquely to the historical suffering of their familial line.[7] Sonny's blues forges an empathic passage through which the narrator's personal loss of self incurred through the loss of his little girl is circumscribed by the losses of self incurred by members of his familial line.

This transference of hidden affect through ritual practice is not just found in Baldwin's "Sonny's Blues." Significantly, Toni Morrison's *Beloved* describes a cultural melancholy that lends insight toward the project of writing African American studies into psychoanalysis and then writing psychoanalysis back into African American studies, two aims this book takes up. Indeed, Toni Morrison's *Beloved* prompts new ways of thinking about the relationship between race and psychoanalysis:

> White people believed that whatever the manners, under every dark skin was a jungle. Swift unnavigable waters, swinging screaming baboons, sleeping snakes, red gums ready for their sweet white blood. In a way . . . they were right. . . . But it wasn't the jungle blacks brought with them to this

place. . . . It was the jungle whitefolks planted in them. And it grew. It spread
. . . until it invaded the whites who had made it. . . . Made them bloody,
silly, worse than even they wanted to be, so scared were they of the jungle
they had made. The screaming baboon lived under their own white skin;
the red gums were their own. (225–26)

Morrison's fictive intervention into the ego's demand to see itself through
biological notions of racial difference renders whiteness and blackness mutually constitutive and thus false projections of a nation struggling to bar
its collective loss of self—that is, its kinship—from recognition. Obsessed
with matters skin deep for far too long, the nation has cannibalized its collective potential. In chapter 2, I demonstrate how the unresolved grief that
remains of disavowed social losses of the past works through current crisis
and struggle, performance, and the process of subject formation to reconstitute itself. Moreover, rather than simply denouncing psychoanalysis as
an arm of the discourse of scientific racism, I try to use its insights about
melancholy to show how August Wilson's *The Piano Lesson* stages parallel
trajectories of psychological restriction sustained by post-Emancipation black
men and women through ritual practice as they struggle for inclusion in a
segregationist society that has historically subjugated them. In doing so, the
chapter extends theories of race and ethnicity by positing a reading of the
racialized subject that shows how that subject is at once constituted through
and distinct from the racial collective and its history of racialization. In doing
so, I want to assert that the multiple and entangled permutations of hidden
affect that attend the disavowed losses of self premised on mass and ongoing
social exclusion and inequality (as opposed to denied "whiteness") allows for
a very particular theorizing of the individualistic and interpersonal character
of racialized subject-formations during the first half of the twentieth century.

The passage from Morrison's *Beloved* quoted earlier provides a perfect
paradigm for understanding how this notion of discreetly reconstituted affect and unmourned social loss move across the racial divide without leaving a trace of its presence to the untrained eye. I am using the term *cultural
melancholy* to describe a ritualized substitution of the visible Other or the
unassimilable with an avowed affective state and a hidden affective state in
which the melancholic couches all s/he has lost and with which s/he cannot come to terms within him/herself. The installation and security of these
mutually constitutive affective states and subject-formations is a psychical
and performative affair; they carry and transform disavowed losses of self
across time and social space through an uneven and contradictory affective
mix—anxiety and entitlement, self-contempt and righteousness, shame and

pride, disgust and desire—and ritual. These rituals of cultural melancholy, I aim to show, work though historical circumstance and conditioned patterns of perception and logic to bolster melancholic subject-formations temporarily.

Through a brief exploration of Anne Cheng's psychoanalytic account of racial melancholy, I would like to discuss further what I mean when I use the terms *avowed affect*, *hidden affect*, and *disavowed loss of self* and how they provide a three-pronged foundation for the dynamic of cultural melancholy. According to Cheng, racial melancholy has two facets; she posits racial melancholia as a complex, ongoing process of racial rejection and desire that shows up in both abject and manic forms:

> On the one side, white American identity and its authority is secured through the melancholic introjection of racial others that it can neither fully relinquish nor accommodate and whose ghostly presence nonetheless guarantees its centrality. On the other side, the racial other (the so-called melancholic object) also suffers from racial melancholia whereby his or her racial identity is imaginatively reinforced through an introjection of a lost, never-possible perfection, and inarticulable loss that comes to inform the individual's sense of his or her own subjectivity. Already we see that these two "sides" are in fact implicated by one another. (*Melancholy of Race*, xi)

Melancholy is part of the process of becoming a racialized subject—which is to say that the disavowal of social loss is what it means to be a racial subject in the world. The relations are necessarily unstable. Racial melancholy establishes itself in relation to the racial melancholy of another subject.

It is precisely this stability and insecurity that renders reconstituted melancholy always present yet hard to trace. By enunciating the properties of melancholy from the standpoint of social losses and their attendant avowed and hidden affects, we are able to account for the multiple and contradictory emotions that characterize race relations and link racialized subject-formations. For the racial melancholic, the lost social possibilities and affect that must be barred from recognition are high maintenance in their unassimilability. As Jacques Hassoun notes in *The Cruelty of Depression*, the social possibilities lost yet disavowed are paired with a mix of emotions that wrestle one another for attention and block one another from "getting the upper hand" (xiii). The affective states thus "smolder under the surface of the sufferer's personality" tinged with a general air of misery and/or unrest (Hassoun, xiii). I hope to show how the social loss nestled discreetly in two layers of affect—both avowed and disavowed—form a trinity of impossible mourning that works through social crisis, ritual, and the process of subject formation to transform and reconstitute melancholy across time and social space.

This study, then, asserts melancholy is an integral element of modern American nationhood that works through fragile racial subject-formations and performances of cultural melancholy to discreetly secure its journey across time and social space. The term "cultural melancholy" also points to how melancholy not only lives a life of the mind but an intersubjective one of culture as well. These rituals are conversational because they place the past and present in dialogue. They are also conversational because they grow out of the competing melancholic states. Moreover, these rituals are conversational because they rely on communal exchange—people talking to and about one another, praying, singing, watching, and listening together— within a particular historical moment. These rituals are cryptic because they transmit and reconstitute disavowed social loss and hidden affect discreetly.

In its concern with the psychical, social, and ideological remains of the dead, my study locates itself within the existing psychoanalytic tradition that underscores the roles of social loss and hidden affect in circumventing and obstructing the process of working through the legacy of racial slavery and neocolonial racism. For example, both Anne Anlin Cheng's *The Melancholy of Race* and Paul Gilroy's *Postcolonial Melancholia* show us not only the importance of exploring the presence of the ghost of imperial and colonial past in everyday political, social, and psychical life, but stress the central role of such insights and reflection in broadening the quality of civic life in our current multiculture "at ease with grievances but not with grief" (Cheng, x). My analysis of the cultural life of melancholy is my book's critical point of departure from these studies. While these studies provide important insight from which my project builds, they generally do not focus on the role performatives play in connecting the past and the present through a ritualized resistance to a normative American nationhood, nor do they ground this legacy in the vectors of power that propel and police America's quest for a state of homogenization in whiteness.

As Gwen Bergner notes, African American literature, literary theory, and psychoanalytic discourse "compress the complex and invisible processes of subject formation into visual crisis" (*Taboo Subjects*, xi). Our enduring relationship with racism and "race" (despite genetic research that debunks biological notions of racial difference), is understood throughout this book as a byproduct of ongoing national and psychic instability, an interplay between the possible and impossible mourning of American nationhood's shared kinship. All this social resistance and performance has left *much that has yet to be seen* behind the scene of difference and thus calls for this project's interdisciplinary engagement with psychoanalysis. In *The Psychoanalysis of Race*, Christopher Lane asserts the idea that "every citizen of Europe and North

America is haunted by the specter of racism" (1). Several scholars in Lane's edited volume directly or indirectly "argue that psychoanalytic accounts of ethnic antagonism not only supplement but potentially are more valuable than historicist critiques of the subject" (2).[8] Indeed, we can no longer afford to exclusively credit discursive and material power as the sole mechanism through which racial antagonism continues to install and mediate subjects. I hope that others will take from my discussion a commitment to accounting for the co-implication of the discursive, the material, and the psychical in the process of racialized subject formation and maintenance. America's racial ideology is at once enmeshed in things material, social, psychical, and performative and, as a result, requires an interdisciplinary interpretive lens for seeing the unseen in the scene of difference. We cannot read the discursive and the material in splendid isolation from the performative and nonrepresentational without perpetuating the hegemony that naturalizes normative social structures and relational codes through denying their co-implication in the first instance. Perhaps it is fitting that my study takes up literary and cultural representations of American modernity as sites of investigation, for it was precisely during this era that America's national discourse of racial and sexual difference merged and the relations between psychoanalysis and socioeconomic history were disavowed (McClintock, *Imperial Leather*, 8).

The coinciding and complementary invisibility of whiteness and visibility of blackness during the early twentieth century is the nation's most undertheorized achievement. The "normal" white moderns who inherited and carried Thomas Jefferson's nationalist mission into the twentieth century did not do so without an intertwined racial, gender, and sexual struggle along the way. Indeed, these gender and sexual struggles were motivated by racism and motivated it. I aim to show how and to what end these sexual and gender struggles in support of white normativity and centrality were negotiated discreetly by way of performatives that manipulated figurations of blackness to infuse white and black racial identifications with inherited and reconstituted melancholy. I also want to assert that attention to the sexual and gender hierarchies that underpin the white majority's melancholic reactions to black enfranchisement's threat to the American myth of cross-class white racial sameness, purity, and promise is indispensable in understanding and resolving the unfinished racial grief work that plagues contemporary American nationhood.

In the introduction to *Female Subjects in Black and White*, Elizabeth Abel, Barbara Christian, and Helen Moglen point out that "As masculinity takes shape in part through its constructions of femininity, whiteness—that elusive color that seems not to be one—gains materiality through the desires and fantasies played out in its interpretations of blackness, interpretations that, by making the unconscious conscious, supplement articulated ideologies of whiteness with less accessible assumptions" (10). In this manner, the editors locate whiteness as an ideological proposition and process that can be fully unpacked only within the context of the ethnic notions and practices upon which it consolidates itself. The current study stages a dialogue between performance studies and theories of melancholia to make further sense of, as Mikko Tuhkanen puts it in *The American Optic,* the raced "subject's emergence as an indelible category of identification and politics even after critical race theory has demonstrated the groundlessness of most racial categorizations" (xii).

The methods and benefits of this critical engagement are complementary. First, the book writes performance studies into critical race studies by way of psychoanalysis in an effort to illuminate how unmourned social loss and hidden grief work through performatives of national belonging and resistance to mobilize relations between and among a catalogue of identity markers—race, ethnicity, gender, sexuality, class, religion, nationality, etc.—to make racial constructions look and feel real. By staging a psychoanalytic and performative reading of "race," we can at once account for the status of race as a constructed category of social difference yet account for the existential complexities of the racialized subject-formation. Second, this study draws on psychoanalysis to broaden performance studies to encompass the project of critical race studies. More specifically, it aims to illuminate how two postmodern playwrights, true to Brechtian form, blur the line between theatergoers and the world of the stage to mourn and resuscitate lost social possibilities secured in the name of racial identification and racism.

Impossible Mourning, the Performative, and the Conservation of Racial Identity

Bringing critical race studies into conversation with performance studies through a consideration of the psychical vestiges of modernity in contemporary processes of subject formation and cultural forms is imperative. The recent work of Diana Taylor recognizes performance as a valid site for the analysis of the ways in which knowledge and identity are transmitted. In *The Archive and the Repertoire,* Taylor outlines the status of performance as an "episteme and practice," stressing the cultural agency that attends the performative event: "Multiple forms of embodied acts are always present, though in a constant state of againstness. They reconstitute themselves, transmitting communal memories, histories, and values from one group/generation to the next. Embodied and performed acts generate, record, and transmit knowledge" (21). That is, embodied practice motivates and is mobilized by knowing and being in the world.

Taylor, for instance, observes that the ongoing media blitz and controversy after the death and funeral of Diana, Princess of Wales, reveal the icon just as active in death. The shrines and tabloid photomontages paying homage to her life, for Taylor, are forms of "performance ghosting" that continue to act politically even as they outstrip life itself. Situating performance as a form of ghosting, Taylor holds that

> [P]erformance makes visible (for an instant, live, now) that which is always already there: the ghosts, the tropes, the scenarios that structure over individual and collective life. These speeches, made manifest through performance, alter future phantoms, future fantasies. (142)

Taylor analyzes the way Diana at once carried on and changed the performance of royalty. For Taylor, embodied practice is a site where the living and the dead comingle, organizing our scenarios of interaction and infusing our sense of self and community with the memories that belong to some other body, place, and time. In this respect, performance intersects the social and political conditions of the past and present. Extending Taylor's insights to racialization and race, we remember, per Anne Pelligrini's recommendation, that the scene of racialization highlights a "painful awareness of who and what may go missing in the scene, and the 'seen,' of difference" (*Performance Anxieties,* 11). How does performance create the very conditions of racial visibility (for people of color) and invisibility (for white subjects) through which the ghosts of American racialization travel across time and social space discreetly? How do these ghosts forge and fortify racial identity in the process?

The critique of racial essentialism without honoring what bell hooks calls "the authority of experience" has been a sticking point for theorists working at the intersections of race and psychoanalysis (*Yearning,* 29). While the "material and cultural paradigms of race and gender that typically frame" African American literary scholarship "effectively describe the external conditions that produce personal experience," Claudia Tate suggests in *Psychoanalysis and Black Novels*, "they cannot explain how individuals internalize or represent those conditions so as to construct personal meaning" (15). Tate asserts that a sustained investigation of the force of desire in black texts "can tell us much about the complicated social workings of race in the U. S. and the representations of these workings in the literature of African Americans" (5). Similarly, Mikko Tuhkanen's *The American Optic* argues for a rereading of race through Jacques Lacan's theory of the Real, suggesting that there is something more to race than its status as a category of social difference. Indeed, the task of reformulating antiquated notions of racial identity and circumventing racism cannot occur in isolation from an account of the complex interplay of social and psychical experience. But as I aim to show in the chapters that follow, the intellectual work of accounting for and moving beyond the Cartesian bifurcations—body versus mind, black versus white—involves a close examination of the process of subject formation at the intersection of multiple categories of social difference and impossible mourning.[9] Extending Tuhkanen's and Tate's insights, this study asserts that an investigation of normative American nationhood's impossible mourning embodied and propagated by performatives provides us with a compelling paradigm for exploring the complexities of modern racial identification and racism. More specifically, in considering the performative and affective conservation of "race," I aim to briefly make sense of the status of race as a constructed yet coherent bodily experience of selfhood, writing performance studies into critical race studies by way of psychoanalysis.

In *The Heart of Whiteness*, Julian Carter observes that "the rise of the notion of the 'normal' to discursive dominance was a crucial part of the process by which whiteness became not only reticent about its racial meaning but blind to its own struggle to retain racial power" (6). Through a detailed reading of popular texts on sex education, childbirth, marital advice, and disease control, Carter admonishes that whiteness rose to the status of "normal" and "supreme" through race-neutral cultural practice. Precisely because normative white male and female subjects worked through cultural practice and figurations of blackness to unwittingly gain subjective stability amidst the ideological crisis of American modernity, an investigation of the avowed and hidden affect and disavowed social loss that attend the social construction of normative American subjectivity provides a fruitful point of critical departure toward achieving the aims of this book.

The demands of American capital and state emancipated the black body from racial slavery only to leverage the body's blackness to fuel its more modern mission of progress through normalization. The decade of the 1850s, according to George Taylor, was characterized by the emergence of the wage earner.[10] In fact, plentiful job opportunity in an urbanizing, industrializing United States brought 1.7 million immigrants into the nation in the 1840s and another 2.6 million in the 1850s. Most of the newcomers entered the working class. And as Taylor notes, for the first time in American history, the wage earners outnumbered slaves and those who worked for themselves. This demographic shift gave birth to the free-labor, antislavery movement that served the emerging capitalist order in the North.[11] This emerging capitalist order subsequently gave birth to a discourse of racial difference that served to support notions of cross-class white racial sameness and promise.

This norming process becomes clear by bringing together claims made by Eric Schocket's reading ("Discovering Some New Race") of Rebecca Harding Davis's 1861 work, *Life in the Iron Mills*. Schocket argues that through a constellation of metaphors, symbols, and imagery, Davis underscores an antebellum discourse of cross-class white racial consolidation and uplift, suggesting that the grim servitude that plagues the white millworkers with pure unmixed blood is a temporary state that will be resolved through what Davis calls "The promise of the dawn" (46–59). Schocket identifies the rise of the industrial revolution and the fall of racial slavery after the Civil War as integral to this process of cross-class and cross-ethnic white consolidation. As Davis's 1864 novella draws to a close, the soot-covered skin of the white millworkers transforms into cadmium white by the light of dawn. In this way, the morphing of the sign of fixed, immutable blackness into a sign of white racial possibility and potential points to the constructed nature of the nation's relatively new cross-class and cross-ethnic white sameness and potential. What *Life in the Iron Mills* provides here is a glimpse into a socioeconomic landscape in which blackness is serviceable to white-skinned members of the U.S. citizenry "on the move." Specifically, Davis's imagery suggests that blackness serves as a disavowed passage through which white working class progress is achieved. Schocket's reading of Davis's parable illuminates the point I aim to make: The journey into and psychical mastery over ethnic notions mobilized and structured the anatomy of the modern American rituals of national belonging and white racial consolidation that rose to popular status during the mid-nineteenth century.

Moreover, the nation's transformation from the era of racial slavery to the post-Reconstruction era exacerbated anxieties generated by the emerging feminist movement of the late nineteenth century and the disruptions of the heteronormative familial structure occasioned by World War I and the Great Depression. It is not without significance that the myth of the black male rapist found reification in popular culture at the same time that the emerging feminist moment exaggerated concerns about white reproductive weakness during the Victorian era. As historian Forrest Wood argues, "For generations, southern white men had successfully dehumanized their women in order to perpetuate their own privileged position and rationalize their own sexual excess. If white women took it upon themselves to express their sexuality fully, the presence of high-powered animalistic negroes would allow them to destroy completely the socio-sexual culture that had evolved throughout the decades" (*Black Scare*, 145).

Charlotte Perkins Gilman's "The Yellow Wallpaper" (originally published in 1892) brilliantly exposes how the Victorians' claim to gentility and reproductive weakness at once reinforced the equation between whiteness and fragility and positioned white heteropatriarchy as the precious purveyor of white bodies and civilization. This short story tells the story of a postpartum woman diagnosed with neurasthenia by her husband, who prescribes the rest cure—isolation and total rest. The story ends on a disturbing note, as both wife and husband go mad in response to the latter's seemingly futile and destructive need to exercise patriarchal control. Gilman's short story provides a vivid illustration of the tenuous relationship between abstract property interests and white heteropatriarchy that ushered U.S. nationhood into the twentieth century.[12] More specifically, John's [the narrator's husband] patriarchal control is motivated by contemporary changes in the value of white racial reproduction. The modern notion Cheryl L. Harris calls "whiteness as property" emerged in this mid-nineteenth century climate.[13] Just as racial slavery ended, the rights and privileges afforded whiteness increased. The gross anxieties over the nation's ideological shift from "slave" and "free" to "black" and "white" as polar constructs in the new, industrial economy to a shift in abstract property interests from the slave's body to whiteness were not managed with ease.

It was precisely the increasing property status of whiteness that at once fueled the "separate but equal" logic of the Supreme Court decision in *Plessy v. Ferguson* (1896) and rendered race something "real and seeable" during the late nineteenth century.[14] In 1892, Homer Plessy, a black yet phenotypically white man, defied Louisiana law by sitting in the train car designated for white passengers. A series of trials and appeals brought Plessy and his lawyers all the way to the U.S. Supreme Court, which held that the races could share citizenship yet conduct "separate but equal" lives. The ruling legislated the racialization of U.S. space mediated through a host of public declarations, namely "No Colored Allowed" and "For Whites Only." This racialization of space aided the conversion of the old, antebellum economic divide between "slave" and "free" into the post-Emancipation economic order of visible racial difference. In doing so, this panoptic terrain of signs and texts worked in concert with the discourse of racial difference to render black bodies social commodities the nation used to secure postbellum white racial uplift and union. Within this context of institutionalized and visual apartheid, whiteness emerged as the national locus of normativity and abstract property of significant value.

The subsequent crisis of uncontained blackness boiled down to a national obsession with preserving a cross-class white ethnic sameness that did not exist in the first place. White heteropatriarchy can be characterized as an ideological-proposition-turned-highest-social-commodity at the dawn of the twentieth century, a nationalist myth produced by the social and economic demands of a nation compelled to disavow the heterogeneity at its core. All of this was reified through social codes and laws of exclusion and, more to my point here, rituals of racialization. The limits and confinement that circumscribed blackness worked through social custom and law to fill whiteness with a host of public and private privileges.

This culture of melancholy was highly stylized. While whiteness was a national fiction, the racial anxiety that produced it was real. This anxiety found its most egregious example of relief in lynching rituals. These performatives drew on figurations of blackness to displace and disavow the white heteropatriarchal vulnerabilities that attended American modernity. These performatives at once threw these racial anxieties into relief and secured the transmission of unmourned social loss through the ritualized process of subject formation and maintenance.

Ralph Ellison's reading of minstrelsy illuminates this dynamic:

> When the white man steps behind the mask of the [blackface] trickster his freedom is circumscribed by the fear that he is not simply miming a personification of his disorder and chaos but that he will become in fact that which he intends only to symbolize; that he will be trapped somewhere in the mystery of hell . . . and thus lose that freedom which, in the fluid, "traditionless," "classless" and rapidly changing society, he would recognize as the white man's alone. ("Change the Joke," 53)

Ellison reminds us that the fear of the Other and the Other within is relieved through a performative objectification and subjection of the Other. Eric Lott elaborates on this dynamic, suggesting that "the minstrel mask itself, offered the experience of 'blackness' even as they absented it" (*Love and Theft*, 100). I read the ritual of lynching as a site where the threat of black paternity and the "miscegenation" normative American nationhood defines itself against, boils up and ebbs in a melting pot of leisure and working-class white possibilities. I read the ritual and spectacle of lynching as a ritual of cultural melancholy, a rite in which a "normal" white working class identity is stabilized through the disavowal of the disremembered realities of sexual relations and homosexuality across the racial divide.

The 4,723 black bodies lynched between 1882 and 1968 reflect more than a fragile racial order stabilized through deadly cultural practice (Daniel T. Williams, "Lynching Records," 5). The double crucifixion of Abram South and Thomas Shipp in 1930, two of scores of lynched and castrated bodies found

FIGURE 1. Double lynching of Abram South and Thomas Shipp
in Marion, Indiana, August 9, 1930. (©Bettmann/CORBIS)

during the era of racial conservatism, represent the remains of a normative, melancholic social body that disavowed its disremembered sexual relations and homosexuality across the color line with great difficulty (see figure 1).

Baldwin's "Going to Meet the Man" illuminates the performative production of a melancholic history of white racial purity by way of figurations of black masculinity and sexuality. Baldwin's short story documents how the lynching and castration ritual is motivated by a disavowed white patriarchal vulnerability and the prohibition against homosexuality. Baldwin's impotent deputy sheriff protagonist, Jesse, unknowingly finds sexual stimulation in past and present acts of violence against black men. In a 1961 interview with Studs Terkel, James Baldwin offers an explanation for the "intolerable anxiety" about racial mixing that characterized American modernity, suggesting that it was rooted in the nation's Protestant Puritan legacy, complete with its patriarchal codes and taboos against sex and the flesh (8). "Going to Meet the Man" is where Baldwin illuminates the essential role the performative plays in this dynamic. Here, the perceived fragility and purity of white womanhood couples with the fear of white male impotence to render the lived and remembered imagery of black male strength and virility an impossible reality Jesse manipulates and manages in the service of his heterosexuality, a constructed identity couched in layers of racial fear and pride.[15]

In describing a lynch mob's difficulty in coming to terms with the bullish resistance of a black man burning at the stake in "Party Down at the Square," Ralph Ellison depicts a similar site of frighteningly possible impossibility. Ellison's narrator recalls the bullish strength of the "nigger": "I was right there, see. I was right there watching it all. It was my first party and my last. God that nigger was tough. That Bacote nigger was some nigger!" (11). Both Baldwin and Ellison subtly locate the lynching ritual as a site where the sign of black male virility is ignited and extinguished. As the lynching and castration scene Jesse remembers suggests, through severing the black man's genitals, "the largest thing [Jesse] has ever seen till then, and the blackest," the lynch mob at once upholds and negates the black patriarchal sign through which the notion of white racial promise and the attendant rights and privileges of citizenship are secured. Readers are also invited to note that such brutal displays of racial antagonism allowed perpetrators to imaginatively co-opt and extinguish black male sexual potency and civic potential.

In *The Black Atlantic*, Gilroy makes an observation I will draw on to make my point clearer: "the culture of diaspora blacks can be profitably interpreted as expressions of and commentaries upon ambivalences generated by modernity and their location within it" (117). In recognizing the distinctive ideological pressures and performative culture that produced and sustained the American union and the myth of white racial sameness, purity, and promise and rendered the black body a knowable entity, this study at once extends and sharpens the focus of Gilroy's critical investigation in *The Black Atlantic*. It does so by locating the black figure of modern U.S. nationhood an ongoing site and source of multiple, overlapping, and competing melancholic states, meanings, and performatives.

Cultural Melancholy treats impossible mourning as an analytic through which to reframe the questions we might pose to Frantz Fanon's scene of interracial contact and racial identification. Providing an imaginative context for exploring the subjective impact of race and racism on the black psychic life, Fanon shares the following in *Black Skin, White Masks*:

> I move slowly in the world, accustomed now to seek no longer for upheaval.
> I progress by crawling. And already I am being dissected under white eyes,

the only real eyes. I am fixed. Having adjusted their microtomes, they ob-
jectively cut away slices of my reality. I am laid bare. I feel, I see in those
white faces that it is not a new man who has come in, but a new kind of
man, a new genus. Why, it's a Negro!

   I slip into corners, and my long antennae pick up the catch-phrases strewn
over the surface of things—nigger underwear smells of nigger—nigger
teeth are white—nigger feet are big—the nigger's barrel chest—I slip into
corners, I remain silent, I strive for anonymity, for invisibility. (116)

An account of the process of racialized subject formation that ignores its
perfomative imbrication with additional social frameworks is only half the
story. This scene is paradigmatic because it clearly points our attention to
the discreet co-implication of the social frameworks and affect—class (progression by crawling), gender (nigger's barrel chest), and sexuality (nigger
underwear smells)—that mobilize racial formation in the process. Here, the
insidious way in which class immobility, the mythology of the black rapist,
and sexual deviance shape black subjectivity and perceptions thereof rise
up into view. More to my point, if, to paraphrase Joseph Roach in *Cities of
the Dead*, there is a strategic "forgetting" (6) that attends the vast and ritualized project of whiteness and, as Carter reminds us in *Heart of Whiteness*,
sexual and emotional "self-control" stand as the core values at the heart of
whiteness (40), we begin to understand the role of the stylized and repetitive
racial encounter (the ultimate performance) in securing the social loss and
hidden affect—that is, the unacknowledged and unresolved gender-, sexual-
ity-, and class-based realities and structures of feeling—that animate racial
identifications. Racial identification is understood throughout this book
as a melancholic performance of class, gender, and sexual choice or affilia-
tion. This culture of melancholy, I aim to show, is mediated by ideological
struggles over the power and privileges associated with "whiteness" against
which a diverse body of white ethnics and minority subjects are measured
and excluded. These identifications of racial belonging and exclusion are
constructed and maintained in the here and now yet stem from unresolved
nationalist grievances that prefigure and outstrip the present moment. This
grieving is deferred imperfectly by the ideological crisis of American modernity. Thus I focus my analysis on the way in which performances of taste,
sensibility, and desire, the burden of racial reclamation, and the illusion of
entitlement and choice carry within and transmit traces of nationalist anxieties over a social history of rape, incest, lynching, homosexuality, sexual
engagement, and birth across its constructed racial divide. This disremembered and disavowed complex stands as the "real and felt" individual and

collective racial experiences and, accordingly, the legacy of racism. Employing a psychoanalytic critique of the performatives of race, this book seeks to restore hidden affect and its ritualized cultural management to its legitimate place in framings of the "real and felt" psychical constraints and dimensions that shape individual and collective racial experiences. Such a critique allows us to account for the sociological facets of race without disregarding "the authority of [racial] experience" (hooks, *Yearning*, 28–29). How, then, do we take grieving into our own hands and move beyond the psychic constraints that continue to overdetermine the interracial encounter in the twenty-first century and, as a result, circumscribe the racialized subject-formation? This book is an extended meditation on this imperative.

One Nation Under Ambivalence

The broadening of performance studies to encompass the project of critical race studies is also imperative. Considering ethnic studies, psychoanalytic theory, and performance studies together opens a gateway to theorizing approaches to loosening the subjective constraints of historical racial grief in the face of contemporary social structures, discourses, and processes that interpellate the subject in kind. While performance studies has not widely embraced race studies and psychoanalytic theory, Kimberly Benston provides such an analysis of Adrienne Kennedy's *The Owl Answers*: "In order to imagine Kennedy's deconstruction of the theatricality of race and gender in another, reconstructive key, black playwrights had first to fully embrace the subversive paradoxes of mediation and difference unveiled by her theater; but they needed to do so, and displace each other in ways that improvise bold new orchestrations of power and desire, history and psyche, experience and expression" (82). Benston goes on to say that Ntozake Shange's *For Colored Girls* stands as a truly fresh dramatization of how performance itself ceaselessly rearranges relations between textuality and history, along with the assumed cognates: understanding and experience, space and time, consciousness and body (83). Benston cites more supple practitioners of the Black Arts Movement who at once open fresh possibilities for "interrogating and formulating African-American self-performance" (79) and staging a mutually defining union with others beyond the black community. In this book, I write from and to discourses of performance theory and psychoanalysis in an effort to uncover how two recent examples of intercultural spectatorship augment racial knowing with racial consciousness by staging racial grief.

Although I cannot here bridge the gaps between critical race studies and performance studies fully, I do want to argue that the psychoanalytic notion of racial melancholy is crucial to advancing performance study's project of undermining the subjective impact of Western paradigms of racial difference and hierarchy. Explicitly characterizing twentieth century intercultural dialogue as a minefield, Diana Taylor shares a model for intercultural communication in the face of overwhelming odds:

> Intercultural or international dialogue is even more difficult and often treacherous. It turns, too often, into power's megalomaniacal monologue with itself. Intercultural communication is not a "thing known," our grid can't frame or capture "it." A praxis rather than an episteme, it can never be assumed; access is never given but always learned . . . the event that brings the past into dialogue with our future, the over there into the here and now. That here and now is not a stable place but a configuration of elements in constant flux. (*The Archive and the Repertoire*, 235–36)

As Amiri Baraka writes, "The revolutionary theater is shaped by the world, and moves to reshape the world . . . it is a social theater" (*Home,* 212). Benston also underscores Baraka's prescient recognition that "the very essence of theater is its immanently collective experience, and in very practical terms, its affirmation or challenge of the audience's codes of conduct, their mechanisms of survival, their shared necessity, outrage, and vision. Theater can tap and redistribute costume and ceremony; it can generate violent energy or neutralize the impulses toward action" (*Performing Blackness,* 36). Indeed, attempts to undo the subjective constraints of racial ideology that ignore the performativity of the interracial encounter itself are insufficient because the psychical resonances of unresolved grief therein are instituted by way of the performative.

The chapters that follow show how and the extent to which the ideological ambivalences of modernity worked persistently through ritual to at once exclude the black body from the privileges of state and capital in the United States and enlist African American cultural resistance efforts to transfer the unmourned social loss and hidden affect that racialized subjects incurred from this history of exclusion across time and social space through the process of subject formation. I have chosen the melancholic subject-formation as a topic for extended study because its ambivalence animates the role performatives play in binding subject-formations to the past and, as a result, opens an analytical passage toward a release from this bondage.

In addition to drawing on discourses of psychoanalysis, critical race studies, and performance studies, *Cultural Melancholy* is a work of cultural and literary studies that draws on and extends queer studies and modernist studies as well. The book engages current debates about the value of psychoanalytic ideas for queer theory by inviting practitioners of the critical approach to reconsider Freud's seminal ideas about sexuality and the unconscious from the perspective of black female same-sex desire. In the process of doing so, I rescue racial, gender, and class distinctions from the atomizing gaze of psychoanalysis and cast them as mutually constitutive dimensions of nation-making and the process of racialized subject formation. *Cultural Melancholy* also challenges the notion that subjects of female same-sex desire acquire sexual identities in isolation from the power dynamics that overdetermine gender and racial subjectivity. The book draws insight from queer race studies to situate the hidden affect and disavowed social loss mobilized by the ritualized construction and normalization of the white, heteropatriarchal familial structure within the context of racial subjugation as the recycled psychic substrate through which minority female same-sex desire is produced and determined. The book thus demonstrates how white-centered psychoanalytic and queer theories have formed a basis for a psychically, materially, and racially contingent theory of female same-sex desire.

This book's central theme of culturally secured and propagated melancholy frames chapter 1, "The Melancholy That Is Not Her Own: The Evolution of the Blueswoman and the Consolidation of Whiteness," where I elaborate on the mutually constitutive nature of the blueswoman's grievances and those of a burgeoning normative social body rife with social loss. This chapter is written in acknowledgement of one of the most enabling moves of recent feminist theory: The exploration of the process of subject formation at the intersections of race, gender, sexuality, and nationhood (hooks, *Yearning*, 57). This chapter argues that if the discourse of racial difference is underpinned by nationalist gender and sexual anxieties, then it makes sense to examine culturally sanctioned figurations of black female sexuality to better understand the psychic legacies of our unacknowledged past of racial segregation and its link to the persistence of racial inequality in our "postracial" moment. Through a close reading of literary and cultural representations of blueswomen, I explore normative American nationhood's reticence about its historical and social construction even as the former absorbs the shock of its social loss and unresolved grief. This cultural field of symbiotic melancholic states provides a context for understanding the co-implication of the material and the psychical in the performance of gender, class, and sexual choices and associations that bolster and stand in for racial identifications discreetly.

Chapter 2, "Reconstituted Melancholy: Impossible Mourning and the Prevalence of Ritual and Race in August Wilson's *The Piano Lesson*," puts psychoanalytic theorizations of Sigmund Freud's concept of melancholia and Jacques Derrida's poststructuralist reading of Karl Marx's work on specters in conversation with Wilson's *Piano Lesson* to take a closer look at the underpinnings of the cultural melancholy that claims post-Emancipation African American subject-formations and cultures. Wilson's play traces racial melancholy sustained and reconstituted as a result of and in resistance to an enduring struggle with racial oppression as American nationhood nestled firmly into the industrial era and normative homogenization and consensus steadily rose against the backdrop of staggering European immigration statistics. Again, rather than simply denouncing psychoanalysis as an arm of the discourse of scientific racism, I try to use its insights about melancholy to show how the play stages parallel trajectories of psychological restriction sustained by post-Emancipation black men and women through ritual practice as they struggle for inclusion in a segregationist society that has historically subjugated them. The chapter extends theories of race and ethnicity by positing a reading of the racialized subject that shows how s/he is at once constituted through and distinct from the racial collective and its history of racialization.

Chapter 3 continues to sketch a grammar for reading the reconstitution of melancholy through a transgenerational process of subject formation. "The Melancholy of Faith: Reading the Gender and Sexual Politics of Testifying in James Baldwin's *Go Tell It on the Mountain* and *The Amen Corner*" takes up the question as follows: How does unresolved racial grief work through the demands of capital, racialization, and sacred ritual practice to enact a gender hierarchy? This chapter thinks through James Baldwin's first novel to explore how testifying serves as a technology of black patriarchy—a ritual that arises out of the need for racial and economic redemption yet unfolds within and propagates gendered power relations. I explore how the content and structure of Baldwin's *Bildungsroman*, set in Harlem's Pentecostal community during the Great Depression, allegorize the conversion of John Grimes, who embodies the "weak, feminine flesh" of his matrilineal line that is sacrificed to secure his "manchild" status of salvation. I read John as the text's metaphor for the feminine flesh of his matrilineal line that is denounced to secure his "manchild" status of salvation—a socially constructed subject-formation, I argue here, rife with the unmourned social loss of the past. This chapter is punctuated by a section that situates Baldwin's novel as a form of sexual testifying on the part of Baldwin himself. In doing so, the chapter places Baldwin's novel in conversation with its dramatic sequel, *The Amen Corner* (1954), to explore how both texts anticipate and extend queer theoretical conversations about the social construction of black, gay subject-formations.

Chapter 4, "Queering Celie's Same-Sex Desire: Impossible Mourning, Trauma, and Heterosexual Failure in Alice Walker's *The Color Purple*," also explores the reconstitution of melancholy at the intersection of race, gender, and sexuality. The chapter also brings the book's critical intervention into queer theory across the racial binary into focus by drawing on psychoanalysis to denaturalize the same-sex desire between two blueswomen. Because of the propensity of psychoanalysis to ground "sexual deviance" within the dynamics of the normative familial drama, many scholars working at the intersection of queer and African American studies have doubted the antiracist potential of psychoanalytic readings of black life. For the most part, the work of such scholars attributes the gender and sexual transgressions within African American culture to socially disorganizing effects of capital and discursive practice.[16] Extending explorations of the black subject-formation at the intersection of material processes, this chapter argues for a sustained analysis that thinks with and through the effects of capitalism and aesthetics, one that explores the resonant inscriptions of the hidden affect and disavowed social loss—that is, the impossible mourning that underpins normative white heteropatriarchy. This chapter places psychoanalytic theories of melancholia in conversation with Walker's *The Color Purple* to show how "deviant" desire is engendered within and maintained by racialized subject-formations, as they are conceived and regulated by the ongoing process of racialization and gender order that guarantees the reproduction of the white heteropatriarchal familial structure that attends a melancholic, normative American nationhood. I wish to explore the transformative possibilities theories of melancholia carry for the intervention into and the interpretation of received fictions of race and sexuality. My rereading of Walker's *The Color Purple* through the psychoanalytic paradigm of melancholia aims to not only depolarize sexual and racial distinctions within the reductive gazes of psychoanalysis and race studies, but also integrates racial difference into the project of queer studies by casting them as mutually constitutive dimensions of the process of subject formation within the broader context of the unconscious processes that attend racialization.

Chapter 5, "A Clearing Beyond the Melancholic Haze: Staging Racial Grieving in Suzan-Lori Parks's *Venus* and Tony Kushner's *Caroline, or Change*," undoes the logic of this study's analytical trajectory, assuming cultural practice is the medium through which we can alter our terms of engagement with the past. This chapter explores how Suzan-Lori Parks's *Venus* and Tony Kushner's *Caroline, or Change* question the impossibility of disaggregating historical racial grief and contemporary race relations by staging racial grief, allowing spectators to locate and mourn the social possibilities lost in the historical and cultural processes mobilized by biological notions of racial difference. This chapter aims to uncover a paradigm for understanding a mode of "theater-based grief work" that merges the racial scene and the racial unseen to prompt theatergoers to mine the hidden affect that structures racial identifications for more discerning and productive terms of engagement across the racial divide.

Cultural Melancholy is at once illustrative and prescriptive: illustrative in that it draws upon psychoanalytic theory to show how unresolved racial grief works through ritual practice to place the living and dead in quiet conversation; and prescriptive because it is in unearthing the nature, permutations, and operations of American nationhood's cultural melancholy that we can throw its unresolved grief into relief and move beyond its devastating effects. For that reason, this study thinks, in response to Sharon Patricia Holland's reminder: "the dead and their relations are perhaps the most lawless, unruly, and potentially revolutionary inhabitants of any imagined territory, national or otherwise."[17] Indeed, *Cultural Melancholy* asserts that keeping company with ghosts can be culturally and politically transformative.

1 THE MELANCHOLY THAT IS NOT HER OWN

The Evolution of the Blueswoman
and the Consolidation of Whiteness

Alberta Hunter: My Castle's Rockin' (2001) documents Alberta Hunter's critically acclaimed return to the blues stage in 1977 after twenty years in retirement. Hunter's career spanned almost the entire twentieth century and her renditions of "Two-Fisted Double-Jointed Rough and Ready Man," "Handy Man," and "Downhearted Blues" continue to soothe and amuse today's blues aficionados.[1] A segment of the documentary depicts the late blues singer serving her traditional dish of double-entendre in "Handyman." While Hunter delivers her lyrics with impeccable timing, the all-white audience responds with laughter and gentle shakes of the head that blur the line between amused identification and judgment of the "out-of-pocket" blueswoman. Two years after Hunter's return to the stage of The Cookery in New York, the show woman received an invitation from President Jimmy Carter to perform for the closing of an annual Governor's Conference at the White House, what was known as Carter's "Mormon Tabernacle." The *Washington Post* reported the following morning: "For last night's black-tie audience, the raunchier the lyrics, the greater the response" (Taylor and Cook, *Alberta Hunter,* 20). The irony here is made palpable by a letter President Carter wrote Hunter the day after: "You continue to amaze us. Rosalynn and I loved your performance last night for the Governors following our dinner in their honor. Thank you for being with us and sharing your beautiful music" (Taylor and Cook, 23).

How did a music born of oppression become the nation's feel-good-soundtrack? How do we explain the process through which the sounds and imagery of black sexuality seeped into normal, everyday American life and leisure? At one extreme are those who attribute the sale of one million copies of Mamie Smith's "Crazy Blues" during its first year in stores to "the ledger"

(Barlow, *Looking Up at Down,* 122). On the other, more sociological, end of explanations, it has been noted that while there was "scarcely a [black] man's name to be found" in the nation's list of blues makers at this time, there are those who attribute the success of the 'Negro female entertainer' to 'the emergence of many white women as entertainers' and the 'great swell of distaff protest regarding women's suffrage'" (Jones, *Blues People,* 93). Another critic pointed out that once the ideal Victorian woman and her notions of "middle-class piety, racial superiority, and sexual repression were discredited," modern America was "free to promote, not an egalitarian society," but a sort of "egalitarian popular culture aggressively appropriating forms and ideas across race, class, and gender lines" (Douglas, *Terrible Honesty,* 8).

In *Black Pearls,* Daphne Duval Harrison draws on biographical and auto-biographical testimonies of both remembered and forgotten blueswomen to explore the overlooked role of black women in the creation and development of the blues and how the cultural form promoted the economic, social, and sexual liberation of black women in a sexist and white supremacist context. Certainly, the classical blues songs by these "blues queens" did much to provide black women with new modes and means of coping with and surmounting the pressures they faced in urban settings. Further, the most popular blueswomen profited handsomely from the patronage of "curious whites who trekked to Harlem in fine cars and furs in search of thrills" (Harrison, 14). Indeed, Alberta Hunter turned to the blues in search of social and economic uplift. As Hazel Carby notes, Hunter and her cohort initially turned to the "clean," well-paying work of singing blues in an effort to escape the debilitating despair of the socioeconomic disenfranchisement they were to inherit as poor, black, single women.[2]

Angela Davis theorized that the blues of black women provided an outlet offering individualization beyond the psychic effects of gender oppression:

> Women's Blues cannot be understood apart from their role in the molding of an emotional community based on the affirmation of black people's— and in particular black women's—absolute and irreducible humanity. The Blues woman challenges in her own way the imposition of gender-based inferiority. When she paints blues portraits of tough women, she offers psychic defenses and interrupts and discredits the routine internalization of male dominance. (36)

The blueswoman's affront to notions of female "place" and its established patterns of subjugation was a critical offensive force for black women living amid a burgeoning imperialist national project in which female challenges to patriarchal authority grew increasingly under fire. During the early twentieth century, Bessie Smith, Ma Rainey, Ethel Waters, and countless other black female blues singers recorded songs for both black and white women.

The trope of the strong, impenetrable black woman made it difficult, however, for mainstream audiences to imagine black bodies assisting the work of advancing American civilization (Davis, 335). Chris Albertson notes the deep-seated racial anxiety that underpinned white America's clamor for black entertainment in the twenties (52). While white show business stars could not afford to expose their unsightly private lives, impropriety and debauchery were prerequisites for black female entertainers of the time. The representational authority of race records and their advertisements linked the problems associated with black female urban sexual behavior to black patriarchy and culture at large. The advertisement for *Rufus Jones for President* (1933), a satirical musical comedy starring Ethel Waters and Sammy Davis Jr., characterized blackness and black domesticity with an ineradicable dysfunction (see fig. 2). Rufus Jones, an African American male child, finds his way to the highest office in the United States. Depicting mouths wide open, eyes boggled, excessive cleavage, and overexposed thighs, the image underscores the musical short's depiction of an unassimilable and dysfunctional black patriarchy. Though merely a two-dimensional print ad for a satirical film, the form and content of both texts loaded the dice against African American political and social life during the Depression era. Working through visual modernity to consolidate biological notions of racial difference, these representations worked in tandem to secure white hegemony.

In the introduction, I argued that the "normal" white modern's struggle for centrality and authority into and through the twentieth century was discreetly negotiated on sexual, gendered, class, and, moreover, performative terms. These struggles were motivated by and mobilized a virulent racism that embroiled figurations of blackness in notions of sexual, gender, and class deviance. Psychoanalytic engagements with social difference have always been intertwined with theorizations of gender and sexual difference. In *"Not Even Past,"* Dorothy Stringer reminds us that white racial fantasies of racial difference cannot be understood in isolation from other categories of social difference. Drawing on Joan Riviere's (1991) theorization of the "womanliness as masquerade" and figurations of black rapist, Stringer points out the fact that Riviere's control case study in this essay was a white, middle-class woman from the southern United States—a successful intellectual, a writer and public speaker who was nonetheless uneasy about intruding on a traditional male field of endeavor. As Stringer argues, the woman's "major strategy for deferring both the rejection she feared, and her own negative feelings, was to assume a 'mask' of womanliness . . . as *not* a direct expression of sexual

FIGURE 2. Advertisement for *Rufus Jones for President* (1933).
(Photo by John D. Kisch/Separate Cinema Archive/Getty Images)

desire, but instead as a psychic translation of their fears about defying gender norms" (24–25). While normative Americans drew on the notion of a "black rapist" to disavow their own gender and sexual transgressions and thus bar the attendant guilt and fear from recognition, the blueswoman's integration into and transformation through American popular culture also served this cultural work.

Serving as a site of sexual and racial crossing for white audience members, the blueswoman's rise to popular status during the interwar period marks the process through which the extreme fear and anxiety that underpinned the lie of racial difference found relief through cultural practice. While the status of the blueswomen as a fixture of popular culture during the early twentieth century was grounded in her controversial embodiment of the phantasm of the "primitive," a trope partly responsible for the normalization of the ideal white modern citizen, her rise to pop-culture status, I argue, was grounded in her status as a cultural underwriter through which normal heterosexuality and whiteness reinforced one another during the Gilded Age.

The ideological work that hinged on the figure of the blueswoman calls for an augmentation of what Roderick A. Ferguson defines as a queer of color analysis in *Aberrations in Black,* adding an account of the workings of unmourned social loss, hidden affect, and performance to the interrogation of "social formations as the intersection of race, gender, sexuality, and class" (149). The nation's ambivalent relationship with the blueswomen was rooted in a larger phenomenon of inevitable nationalist change and accommodation by which the capitalist circulation of figurations of blackness solidified the color line amid a fragile ideological field of unstable class, ethnic, gender, and sexual identifications. The task before us is to illuminate the disavowed psychic underpinnings and cultural effects of this liaison between the blueswoman and white audiences. Indeed, literary and cultural representations of the performances and lives of African American blueswomen and blues culture reveal something beyond normative American nationhood's reticence about its historical and social construction. How did the blueswoman unwittingly aid in the construction of the nationalist myth of the cross-class white racial sameness, purity, and promise? How did this ideological work of blues culture evolve into a sort of racial violence against white ethnics and black enfranchisement at once? What is the role of racial melancholy, a concept virtually missing from understandings of 1920s and 1930s black performance, in the evolution of popular performances of the cultural form as it "correspond[ed] with and diverge[d] from nationalist ideals and practices" (Ferguson, 149)?

The Disavowed Buttressing of Whiteness through Black Culture

Making large psychological and ideological claims about white racial identity requires first defining what it is, and recent cultural theory has done just that. "'Normality,'" wrote Julian B. Carter in the introduction to *The Heart of Whiteness*, "provided a common, and deeply sexualized, vocabulary through which an increasingly diverse group of whites could articulate their common racial and political values to one another, while nonetheless avoiding direct acknowledgment of or confrontation with the many hierarchies that fractured the polity" (6). What exactly does Carter mean by "deeply sexualized vocabulary"? More significantly, how does such a vocabulary achieve its effects without direct acknowledgment, debate, and race politics? This discourse of racial difference, Carter argues, was camouflaged and policed by a depoliticized discourse of "normal" sexual desire and behavior. Justifying this controversial study of race, Carter explains:

> In common speech during the interwar years, "normality" described a whole series of ideals regulating sexual desires and activities and, through them, modes of intimacy and familial structures. By 1940, this enframement had had the effect of helping to expand white racial definition to include most European Americans who adhered to these racialized sexual and relational norms. Erotically and affectively charged marriage became the privileged site for the literal and metaphorical reproduction of white civilization. At the same time and through the same gestures, that civilization's core racial value was redefined in terms of love. (6)

Carter's provocative linkage between the disavowed regulation of sexual desire and activity and the reproduction of white civilization allows us to look more closely at the reticent cultural work responsible for the mutually dependent racial and sexual hierarchies that at once commodified and made whiteness invisible.

During the era between the two world wars, the discourses of "civilization" and "normality" intersected and overlapped to relegate the work of advancing and populating America's civilization to the domain of white men and women. By 1940 "normality" took the place of "civilization," transferring "civilized Americans" into a broader, more inclusive category of "normal Americans." While the conceptual content of both terms performed the same cultural work, Carter argues, the latter achieved these ends without political debate. Once the notion of "civilized and well-bred" bourgeois Protestant whites was decentered and replaced by the need for a more inclusive national self-image consistent with an ethnically diverse white racial repub-lic, the myths of scientific racism were augmented with a more everyday nationalist culture of regulation. Carter's argument is grounded in a set of diverse sources—descriptions of modern nervousness, sex advice for mar-ried couples, and educational materials about reproductive physiology and venereal disease—which all "speak about sex from and to the position of civilized modern whiteness" (18).

This culture of regulation, of course, prompts a few pertinent questions: what is "normal"; what is "deviant"; and through what cultural and psychic forms and conditions does the former constitute the latter, and vice versa? For Carter, the internal focus of the popular-science sources that developed a definition of "normality" that centered white racial marital romance as the desirable mode of white civilization's reproduction required the refusal of the sexually and racially nonnormative subject's claim to civilization. Countless studies have explored the ways in which the core at once defines and mediates itself through excluding and rendering the periphery invisible. Moreover, the role bodies on the margins play in mediating the sexual desire and activity of the center—thus, defining the center—is never discussed in terms that register the interplay of performance, unmourned social loss, and hidden affect. What is missing from studies of the blues culture and critical race studies is knowledge about how the normative social body appropriated representations of the cultural form to power a culture of sexual and social regulation that secured its hegemony. The psychoanalysis of jazz and blues offers an elegant means of writing performance studies into the project of critical race studies, addressing the difficult relationships among racial iden-tities, categories of social difference, and performance. Knowledge of the ideological underpinnings of the unmourned social loss and hidden affect that mobilized jazz and blues cultures provides a grammar for reading race as less biological and more of a performative construction of belonging and intimacy at the intersections of class, sexual, and gender difference.

Flesh That Moans in the Age of Racial Conservatism

Psychoanalytic studies have drawn usefully on the concept of melancholia to theorize the stable yet fragile structures of racial, gender, and sexual iden-tification.[3] Judith Butler's theorization of gender performativity points to the ways embodied behaviors, speech acts, and other cultural forms fortify and constrain fragile melancholic states and their constitutive social losses (*Psychic Life of Power*, 132–50). Of course, as Stuart Hall reminds us, cultural identity is an act of being and becoming.[4] But why and how does this happen? A rearticulation of critical studies on blackface minstrelsy through the prism of racial melancholy, suggests that working-class Irish actors and audiences who worked through the popular ritual to become more self-consciously white were unknowingly masking their own gender and sexual particularities as a result of cultural prohibitions against miscegenation and homosexuality. Indeed, the popular cultural form facilitated a crossing and policing of the racial divide on disavowed gender and sexual terms and conditions.

Scholars of blackface minstrelsy stress the racial crossing component of the cultural form, and they are quick to point out "that immigrants at times developed significant contacts with Black culture" (Roediger, *Working Towards Whiteness*, 188). Understanding social identity as a melancholic construction helps us read the movement of the immigrant in blackface steadily toward normative American identification in the image of blackness as a sort of misrecognition of the gender and sexual particularities veiled beneath their image of whiteness. According to Eric Lott in *Love and Theft*, on the one hand, the fantasy of racial crossing enacted in blackface seems to gesture at once toward sexual envy toward and desire for black men. On the other hand, the minstrel's identification with potent male heterosexuality deflected latent homosexual desire. At base, the cultural form was a melancholic strategy through which "normal" white working class identity is stabilized through the ritualized and disavowed engagement with and containment of the threat of miscegenation and homosexuality.

While much of the scholarship on the spectacle of minstrelsy revolves around the Americanization of the working-class white immigrants who engaged in the cultural form during the late nineteenth century, little has been said about the modern sites of popular culture designed to secure white psychic subjection long after minstrelsy's fall from the popular stage. Picking up where minstrelsy left things, the nation's relationship with the blueswoman is deeply embroiled in this early twentieth century cultural imperative. The social history between the blueswoman and early twentieth century white racial subjects clamoring for national belonging is at once contradictory and complementary. The three decades before the term "heterosexuality" gained common usage and, in turn, mobilized the construction and consolidation of "normal" whiteness in the 1940s, white moderns enlisted the mass culture of visual modernity to align themselves with primitivism associated with black and immigrant bodies to promote the masculine yet refined superiority of "civilized" men. (See Bederman, esp. 213–15.)[5] During the 1920s, gender ideologies conflating white male power with self-restraint were under serious scrutiny and reconstruction. Victorian repression, after all, was not only an offense against human nature; it was an ideological error of the past that threatened the future of well-bred Anglos.[6] In fact, figurations of the black primitive were deployed by white men to aid them in their efforts to revive the evolutionary progress of the race by inoculating their Victorian civility with a healthy measure of sexual deviance.

In the 1924 work "The Caucasian Storms Harlem," Rudolph Fisher offers a thought-provoking description of this cultural buttressing of white hegemony through figurations of blackness:

> But suppose it is a fad—to say that explains nothing. How came the fad? What occasions the focusing of attention on this particular thing—rounds up and gathers these seasonal whims, and centers them about the Negro? Cabarets are peculiar, mind you. They're not like theatres and concert halls. You don't just go to a cabaret and sit back and wait to be entertained, you get out on the floor and join the pow-wow and help entertain yourself. Granted that white people have long enjoyed the Negro entertainment as a diversion, is it not something different, something more, which they bodily throw themselves into Negro entertainment in cabarets? "Now negroes go to their own cabarets to see how white people act." . . .
>
> This interest in the Negro is an active and participating interest. It is almost as if a traveler from the North stood watching an African tribe-dance, then suddenly found himself swept wildly into it, caught in its tidal rhythm. (1243)

Fisher casts the Harlem cabaret as a recreational destination for the downtown emigrants. The rhythmic sounds of the cabaret provide an unmediated empathic passageway toward a deeper vitality by way of figurations of blackness. Fisher's narrator notes that the voices of blueswomen like Ethel Waters were admired for their "characteristically African" tenor that could "make a preacher lay his bible down" (1237). The implication here is palpable: This blueswoman's rhapsodies in black were seductive, providing white listeners with empathic currency toward more sensual bodily investments. The fervent desire for these rhapsodies in black serve as placeholders for the Victorian culture of sexual restraint that cannot be avowed and the accompanying amusement covers the general despair of "civilized" men and women. Small's Paradise in Harlem was one of many venues where "deviant" modern whites worked through the sexual anxieties and tensions of their time. But how could the modern white woman complement this reformulated white manliness and still retain the femininity, restraint, and protection against the black male phallus upon which the progress and maintenance of modern white civilization depended?

One of the key features of modern culture is that it characteristically changed to allow white moderns to work through the social tensions of their time. The blueswomen's evolution into the jazzwoman that rose to popular status during the Depression era points more to the ingenuity dominant culture employed to capitalize on normative America's crisis of white ethnic diversity than its embrace of the nation's black citizenry. While the early twentieth century remaking of manhood hinged on figurations of black male primitivism, the project of remaking modern white patriarchy relied on a more assimilated urban black culture. These cultural forms served to discipline white heteropatriarchal conduct in matters of the heart, marriage, and reproduction as race-specific subjects and activity. The blueswoman's growing popular status was grounded in mass culture's ability to redress and market her racial, gender, and sexual difference at the same time as the more inclusive panethnic category of "Caucasian" began to overshadow the hierarchically organized and increasingly problematic categories of white ethnic diversity that prevailed throughout most of the nineteenth century.[7] Initially, the blueswoman's mythic gender and sexual excess provided a disdainful edge upon which well-bred white Anglos could sharpen their self-definition or a vehicle of melancholic cultural embodiment. The nation's eventual attachment to the blueswoman's more tempered expressions of sexual desire and discipline in the form of swing worked to mobilize and police the reproductive ends of "normal" white moderns who systematically denied her the privileges of normality she helped to shape. Of course, all of this occurred in cross-racial scenes and atmospheres of happiness and bliss that made it easy for white moderns to evade engagement with racial inequality and the attendant racial anxieties.

It is no wonder why the ghosts of the age of racial conservatism continue to haunt contemporary race relations in the United States. The widely held and progressive view that race is a social construct tells us little about why racism persists even in contexts where there is no social privilege or power to gain. One way to understand this phenomenon is to analyze the way racial melancholy works through popular cultural forms and practice to mobilize white racial identifications that stand in as avatars for the gender and sexual anxieties that at once have nothing to do with yet are intertwined with figurations of blackness. To date, cultural criticism provides no direct comment about the figure of the blueswoman at the intersections of private and public experience. It is important to situate the cultural figure as the nationalist and original melancholic object through which the gender, sexual, and class anxieties that underpinned modernity's color line shaped white racial experiences of self-in-the-world without a trace. This lack of critical engagement with the cultural work of unresolved racial grief is one of the vestiges of modernity's investment in the visual practices and technologies used to secure biological notions of racial difference. This investment in race could not have achieved the widespread disavowal of the shared kinship between blacks and whites in isolation from a melancholic culture of affilia-tion and choice designed to maintain this denial through the accumulative social and psychological effects of ritual and everyday practice. These social losses could not be mourned in the name of providing a diverse body of white ethnics a cover of normality, biological polarity in relation to blackness, and promise in a discreetly segregated caste system within the ranks of whiteness. The story of Billie Holiday lays bare this culture of melancholy during the interwar period. All of this melancholic cultural work, I aim to show, staged Holiday's tragic death and lives discreetly with us, directing our private and public traffic. Let us begin this journey of self-discovery and racial mourning with F. Scott Fitzgerald's *The Great Gatsby*, published in 1925.

Jazz Scenes, White-Ethnic Mixing, and the Consolidation of Well-Bred Anglo Purity in *The Great Gatsby*

"As we crossed Blackwell's Island a limousine passed us, driven by a white chauffeur, in which sat three modish negroes, two bucks and a girl. I laughed aloud as the yolks of their eyeballs rolled toward us in haughty rivalry. 'Any-thing can happen now that we've slid over this bridge,' I thought; 'anything at all. . . .' Even Gatsby could happen, without any particular wonder" (Fitzger-ald, *The Great Gatsby*, 69). In one private reflection, Nick Carraway, the narrator of F. Scott Fitzgerald's *The Great Gatsby*, frets over a socially un-stable American modernity. The plot follows a man, Jay Gatsby, who tries and fails to change his social standing by marrying the lost love of his life, Daisy Buchanan. Their desire for one another is unrequited because Gatsby's upper-class standing is a necessary yet insufficient qualification for winning Daisy's well-bred Anglo hand in marriage. While Gatsby's white racial ob-scurity during the 1920s promised to link him to the emerging monolithic "Caucasian" racial category by the 1940s, his mysterious origin ties him to the gender and sexual particularities that threatened the self-discipline that underpinned the WASP moral and political ideal. While Gatsby's social excess is everything Daisy desires in her husband, Tom Buchanan, the sweetheart she truly desires, lacks what is perceived as high lineage biological white-ness. For Nick, the mere possibility of Jay Gatsby's grasp of privilege and power is a sign of unprecedented changing times—emerging, that is, from industrial capitalism's redistribution of the nation's wealth beyond the hands of well-bred Anglos. As a consequence, the economic inequality within the ranks of whiteness that historically fortified well-bred white supremacy was losing its force, particularly in the nation's urban centers. At the same time, Jay Gatsby's relative popularity, powered by his swinging jazz parties, marks his embodiment of the very racial eroticism that once policed the color line within the ranks of whiteness.

Like jazz, the racial and sexual brew Gatsby signifies at once challenges and reinforces the nation's renewed investment in white heteropatriarchy during the interwar period. Indeed, the rise of black culture to mainstream status during what is also known as the Jazz Age was facilitated through a national-ist push to construct, as Carter notes in *Heart of Whiteness,* a more modern brand of white heteropatriarchy that replaced Victorian sexual restraint with a gendered sexual discipline. Indeed, the novel lays bare how the collapse of blackness into mainstream popular culture during the era occasioned an extension of the gender and sexual particularities that once bracketed black-ness into a fringe domain of white ethnicity that further consolidated and privatized the privilege of a well-bred Anglo center. Ultimately, the novel brings into sharper focus the status of whiteness as an ideological proposition and process that enlisted the nation's racial heterogeneity to instantiate and police an ideal white normative center as it expands the margins of normativ-ity. In the process, we see how the national myth of cross-class white racial sameness, purity, and promise became a national desire, leaving melancholic hope and aspiration in the place where the social construction of whiteness might be acknowledged and the resulting social loss mourned. We also bear witness to how the inability to mourn this absent sign and move beyond its cloak of righteousness rendered blackness a proxy for sexual, gender, and class alterity.

Jazz scholars of the interwar period, such as Lewis Erenberg and Chris-topher Small, frame the Jazz Age as a time when the social aberrations that threatened ideal manhood and womanhood amid the ravages of war also gave birth to a conservative movement bent on diffusing these challenges. At the same time, there was a need in white culture for the emotional honesty black culture had to offer as the war undercut the idea of restraint of the passions for social duty.[8] In *Bessie*, Chris Albertson identifies a need for ventilation that underpinned white elite engagement with black culture: "They saw blacks as happy-go-lucky people who laughed infectiously, showed an enviable lack of restraint, and really understood how to have a good time. So white elites came, laughed, sinned, and slipped back into their Tiffany world before the first rays of dawn struck the ghetto" (137–38). These refractory moments amid massive transformation and racial tumult most profoundly illustrate a ritualized construction of two new pillars of ideal whiteness: the "man of morale" and the sexually-engaged-yet-self-disciplined white female.

Greg Forter in "Against Melancholia" suggests that the fight against the feminizing effects of modernity gave way to a new form of manhood that "sought to root out the femininity that had once served to balance male aggression. Manliness was now to be unambiguously hard, aggressive, physically dominative, potent—and this version of manhood was then projected back into the past, imagined as a primal essence eclipsed by a feminizing modernity that it was now the business of man to combat" (145). According to Forter, *The Great Gatsby* is representative of a dominant strand of American modernism that responds melancholically to the disavowed social loss of a "masculinity that combined aggressiveness and competitive rigor with the gentler, more 'feminine' qualities of self-restraint, moral compassion, and the cultivation of interior virtues" (144). Forter argues that the novel teaches the limits of a melancholy politics by showing us how Fitzgerald displaces the hostile components of his melancholic ambivalence onto convenient scapegoats—that is, women and effeminate men:

> The residual manhood figured by Gatsby represented for him [Fitzgerald] an identificatory possibility, a way of living one's masculine identity that felt at least potentially viable; in destroying that possibility, capitalist modernity had severed Fitzgerald from vitality expressive components of the self. The ambivalence activated by that loss—an ambivalence resulting from his having internalized the emergent hostility to femininity—was therefore also directed inward. *Gatsby's* redirection of this ambivalence onto women can then be seen as an aesthetic strategy for managing a potentially suicidal self-aggression, but managing it in a fashion the misogyny of which should be clear. . . . Furthermore, inasmuch as the loss of residual manhood entailed the loss of expressive intimacies *between men*—Fitzgerald wrote in his *Notebooks* that "the fairies [had] spoiled" such intimacies (no. 62)—we can supplement my reading so far by saying that the novel's melancholic strategies are also a historically specific enactment of the psychic process described by Butler. Fitzgerald aesthetically embalms Gatsby as an always already lost possibility in part to defend against a homosocial love that he yearned to express but felt could no longer be distinguished from homosexual desire. (163)

If gender and sexual hierarchies motivated and were mobilized by the discourse of racial difference, then the melancholic logic that ultimately propels the plot of *The Great Gatsby* turns on the disavowal of the white racial self-governance—that is, the cultural melancholy—that underpins the myth of cross-class white racial sameness, purity, and promise. While Foster reads Gatsby himself as an effect of Fitzgerald's concern with a crisis of masculinity posed by the modern marketplace, the fate of Gatsby, I suggest, is an effect of Fitzgerald's concern with a corollary crisis in white American racialization.

The feminizing effects of modernity were at once experienced and alleviated on racial terms. The general anxiety about the feminizing effects of modernity on white masculinity were exacerbated by the rising number of African Americans and immigrants flooding the nation's urban centers during the early twentieth century. As the second stage of capitalist production—monopoly capitalism—thwarted white male self-making through bureaucratic structures, rising black and immigrant agency and competition in the workplace solidified widespread consensus about white emasculation. Moreover, it began to seem as if the African Americans and immigrants were displacing "overcivilized" white male authority. And so, as Small reminds us, "there was a need in white culture for what the black culture had to offer, and that, equally, the majority of white people dared not to confront that culture directly but needed to diffuse the challenge it posed to their own culture and value" (*Music of the Common Tongue,* 149). For that reason, it's not whimsical to say jazz was born out of the very same racial conflict it was eventually enlisted to camouflage. During the 1920s, jazz emerged as a new form of popular culture that worked through sound and performance to inoculate white moderns with the emotional and physical honesty associated with blackness.

This social history helps us extend Forter's reading of the social loss crystallized and unmourned in the figure of Gatsby. Fitzgerald seemingly grasped his outsider-insider status in the ranks of whiteness and how the status of well-bred Anglos hinged on their ambivalent relationship with social excess that modernity forced them to endure. Indeed, Fitzgerald seems to have experienced the fall of Gatsby and his jazz scene as the disavowed jeopardy of cross-class white ethnic identity status. Like Gatsby, Fitzgerald's white racial identity, on one hand, offered the promise of cross-class white racial sameness. On the other hand, Fitzgerald and Gatsby's white racial identification was not enough to secure well-bred, white Anglo-Saxon status.

Gatsby's destruction marks the disavowed intraracial governance that attends the social construction of a normative white modern and a nationalist disavowal of the mythic status of cross-class white racial sameness and promise. Again, while Jay Gatsby's white racial obscurity during the 1920s promised to link him to the normative racial category by the 1940s, his mysterious origins tie him to the gender and sexual particularities that threatened the self-discipline underpinning WASP moral and political ideals. During a time when the U.S. government placed limits on immigration, the number of African American emigrants from the South living in the North peaked, and gender order experienced reconfigurations, Daisy Buchanan's sexual propriety stands as the promise and precious jewel of white civilization. Almost a decade shy of Jess Willard's reclamation of the title of heavyweight champion of the world from Jack Johnson, Tom Buchanan is invested fully in his duty as a white man to protect the white race and, as a result, civilization from the threat of submersion. At the same time, contemporary changes in the meaning of gender suspend Daisy somewhere between proprietor and custodian of her virtue. Daisy's decision not to honor her love for Gatsby and, at the same time, leave him with a naïve hope for their union is a melancholic affair. More specifically, the decision and the false hope it leaves behind situate white racial identification a value proposition with an unacknowledged sliding scale of returns for its investors.

Fitzgerald provides a literary reenactment of how the jazz scenes Gatsby sponsored served as reiterative melancholic strategies through which white ethnics secured their social and psychic investments in whiteness through figurations of blackness under false pretenses. The novel confronts readers with the nonpoliticized contexts that cultural figurations of blackness like jazz provided for well-bred white Anglo Saxons to exercise gendered and sexual self-governance and police their bloodlines in spite of the expanding spectrum of white ethnicity that formed normative American nationhood during the interwar period. The narrator's sobering statement—"They were careless people, Tom and Daisy—they smashed up things and creatures and then retreated back into their money or their vast carelessness, or whatever it was that kept them together, and let other people clean up the mess they made" (180–81)—points to the ideological refuse generated and passed on by fiscally conservative indifference.

Billie's Swing and the Nation's Adjustment Without Improvement

Thus far, the theoretical thrust of this chapter lies in its concern with the role black cultural expressions played in constructing and buttressing the ranks of whiteness. What effect did this culture-based ideological work have on black lives? We know this cultural work hinged on the notion of a black racial essence. Beginning with the first slave narratives written by Africans in America, the most marketable texts were narrated directly from personal experience. This self-objectification at once paved the route to freedom and supported notions of racial essentialism that haunt our contemporary multiculture. As Kenneth Mostern reminds us, "The belief in some kind of racial essence has been perfectly compatible with advocacy of integrationist positions" (*Autobiography and Black Identity Politics*, 21). Holiday's "Strange Fruit" circulated in a post–World War America in which legalized exclusion, racial segregation, and stereotypes of African Americans as roving rapists and prostitutes dominated the national imagination. We must look no further than the legislated ban on interracial marriage and sex between members of different "races" to account for the 4,723 black bodies lynched between 1882 and 1968.[9] Dorothy Stringer has recently given historical depth to this crisis, noting "the 'Southern Rape Complex' is continually reproduced and rearticulated, even in the absence of its material support, even in the literal absence of African American men" (*"Not Even Past,"* 35).

Considering the conservative racial ideology that dominated the first quarter of the twentieth century, Holiday's rise to fame during the era seems ironic. In fact, Holiday herself was rumored to be a prostitute, the antithesis of the "cult of true womanhood" that relied on racist figurations of black degeneracy. Midway through Diana Ross's portrayal of Billie Holiday in Sidney Furie's *Lady Sings the Blues* (1972), viewers witness an unprecedented representation of black female identity in the U.S. public sphere. Furie's Holiday embodies the "cult of true womanhood," a status reflected mostly in the manner in which she delivered song. Holiday's tenure with both Count Basie and Duke Ellington's bands, the "swingin'est band[s] in the land," provided the context for her to master the ability to make her words swing elegantly.[10] Encouraging audiences to "tap deep springs of hope, peace, and passion," swing as a genre provided singers like Holiday opportunities for much economic advancement" (O'Meally, *Lady Day*, 43). The film depicts a Holiday who revised the black Jezebel myth, a beautiful African American woman who sings about affectively charged marriage with perfect pitch. On the surface of things, Holiday seems to undermine the racial ideology that bars black bodies from the privileges of American state and capital, a transgression she executed with great precision. Holiday's acoustic management seemingly allowed her to transcend her corporeal limits. In a compelling reading of *Lady Sings the Blues* (1972), Lindon Barrett considers the value of film representations in light of the blueswoman's negotiations across social boundaries and borders, noting that boundaries are surreptitiously transgressed by social figures "sited (sighted) outside of value and, because this site (sight) without value amounts to the (sight) where boundaries do not prevail, it is from this vantage . . . that one can most keenly revise and redress the formalized boundaries of value" ("In the Dark," 882). Holiday's position grounded in sound (without boundaries) allows her to "undertake another production of value," a value without boundaries (882). Sound is a medium that defies boundaries regardless of those placed in the site (sight) of its source. Barrett adds: "From Holiday's vantage that is inscribed in sound and by the singing value, the site (sight) without boundaries are rendered very different from customary American rehearsals" (882). While scholars have attributed this variance to the growth of a more egalitarian popular culture, the story of Billie Holiday suggests this is more of a social adjustment without improvement. Indeed, the growing popularity of jazz culture during the 1920s worked through the swing ballroom and radio to place the blueswoman behind the doors of white domesticity. However, Holiday's sound was culturally melancholic. Its sophistication served a nationalist imperative: consolidating white racial marital bliss and promise. It also excluded her insidiously from the privileges and promise of whiteness, leaving her with unrequited desire and unfathomable layers of social loss at once. After all, while the body supplanted by the promise of sound loses its abject status in the economy of observation, sound gives way to less overt yet pernicious forms of racial antagonism. At first probe, one might say that the interracial climate here is an innocent one, an involuntary, "normal" current in the direction of a more progressive American life. However, as Jacques Attali reminds us in *Noise*, something as "normal" as sound is far from innocent, so intricately woven into the fabric of everyday life that its power is ubiquitous and hard to see.[11]

In her autobiography, Holiday depicts the swing ballroom as a place where white patrons paid for performances of disembodied blackness:

> They came to the Cotton Club—a place Negroes never saw inside unless they played music or did the shakes or shimmies. But these were just side shows specially set up for white folks to come and pay their money for kicks. These places weren't for real. The life we lived was. But it was all backstage, and damn few white folks ever got to see it. When they did, they might as well have dropped in from another planet. Everything about it seemed to be news to them. It was rugged. Sometimes I wonder how we survived. But we did. (Holiday, *Lady Sings the Blues*, 46–47)

Mainstream America's interest in Billie Holiday's artistry was grounded in its status as a medium for working through the white racial fears and anxieties that accompanied modernity's increasingly rigid social mandates and possibilities for white manhood and womanhood. Holiday used her very short range to appease a mainstream audience increasingly concerned with finding personal and racial security in love. As Carter reminds us, the more white moderns talked up their "heterosexuality," the less they needed to claim "ideal whiteness" (*Heart of Whiteness*, 98). Without knowing the ideological implications of her artistry yet fully aware the future of the whole band was in her hands, Holiday delivered songs with force and measured restraint: "When I ended the number I held onto the word 'ain't,' then I held 'no,' then I held my breath, thinking the jury was out and wondering what the verdict would be, and I sang the word 'swing.' I hadn't got the word shaped with my mouth when people stood up whistling and hollering and screaming and clapping" (*Lady Sings the Blues*, 84).

With songs like "What You Gonna Do When There Ain't No Swing?" and "Them There Eyes," Holiday stimulated the reproductive goals of white heteropatriarchy, providing an elaborate string of metaphors that privatized thoughts of pleasure while serving the reproductive values and consolidation goals of white heteropatriarchy. "These were songs that helped a generation endure the trials of Depression—not just with otherworldly fantasies, though she offered a few of those, too, but with danceable music that was alive with the quicksilver sound of a richly inventive artist exuberantly at work" (O'Meally, *Lady Day*, 117). The fact that Holiday's star rose when the racial and relational ideal was reshaped in more inclusive terms of normality that promised citizenship to an increasingly diverse white ethnic population is not without significance. The rhythm of swing became the soundtrack of a nation growing increasingly reticent about the gender, sexual, and class terms that underwrote its white racial norming sessions during the interwar period.

Carter describes how "Normality drew on and extended several earlier complicated vocabularies, especially those of civilization and evolution, in a way which made it possible to talk about whiteness indirectly, in terms of the affectionate reproductive heterosexuality of 'normal' married couples. That is, 'normality' made it possible to discuss race and sexuality without engaging the relations of power in which they were embedded and through which they acquired much of their relevance" (*Heart of Whiteness*, 3–4). All of this happened amid the inclusive imagery of a racially tolerant republic. Unwittingly, blueswomen of the era of big swing worked through sight and sound to secure the centrality and authority of a growing heteropatriarchal familial structure. And all of this occurred through a nonconfrontational and race-neutral discourse of love, gender order, and class mobility that encouraged white spectators to elude engagement with the virulent racism and inequality that existed just beyond the music-hall door. Together, the images illustrate how the pleasures of swing music served as screens through which the despair over Depression-era racial inequality was covered to secure a diverse body of white ethnics in heterosexual whiteness. Figure 3 stands out for the nostalgia-inducing quality of the photograph, the innocence of the

FIGURE 3. Billie Holiday in performance (circa 1930s).
(Photo by Harry Hammond/V&A Images/ Getty Images)

event, and the look of appreciation on the faces of the audience members. The photograph frames Holiday beyond the boundaries of Depression-era racial and economic strife; the irony of her ideological subjugation amid the "high life," however, is made palpable. Margaret Bourke-White's famous photograph of African Americans standing in line at an emergency relief station in the aftermath of an Ohio flood in 1937 (Figure 4), when the Depression was in full force, highlights the racially segregated "American way" Holiday supported through race-neutral themes and song. In this way, Holiday's stimulation of affectionate and disciplined reproductive heterosexuality served to both challenge traditional stereotypes of African American women and supported the intimacy of "normal" married couples linked by their disavowal of the social injustice their cohesion instigated.

This is not to say that the swing ballroom, representing the interstices of the racial divide, was not a site where the nation's primary melancholic

FIGURE 4. African American flood victims line up to get food and clothing from a Red Cross relief station in front of a billboard extolling "World's Highest Standard of Living" (circa 1930s). (Photo by Margaret Bourke-White/ Time & Life Pictures/Getty Images)

retention—that is, biological notions of racial and social difference—broke down and gave way to extreme forms of racial anxiety. Indeed, white racial indifference is an unstable melancholic state that gives way to rage, anxiety, or both, affective buffers against its own collapse and the realization of the fictional status of white racial sameness, purity, and promise. Holiday's life on stage with white men unnerved some patrons who reduced the interracial liaison to "taboo" sexual engagements. Hotel managers catered to these racial anxieties, forbidding Holiday to mix with white customers and enter through the front door. Unable to come to terms with Holiday's approximation of the white racial ideal, a ballroom audience levies the force of the racial binary: "Next they told Basie I was too yellow to sing with all the black men in his band. Somebody might think I was white if the light didn't hit me just right. So they got a special dark grease paint and told me to put it on" (O'Meally, *Lady Day,* 68).[12] While audiences received their fill of Holiday's dream sequence of regulated desire, affection, and intimacy, the singer performed to ward off looming feelings of social indignity. This burden of racial reclamation is a culturally induced yet "real and felt" experiential component of racial identification. Recounting the price of her fame, Holiday laments, "It wasn't long before I was one of the highest-paid slaves around. I was making a thousand a week—but I had about as much freedom as a field hand in Virginia a hundred years before" *(Lady Day,* 121). While the singer's well-publicized addiction to heroin was symptomatic of authority's melancholic attachment to biological notions of racial difference, Holiday's ability to deliver performances with perfect pitch in spite of her pain and bitterness suggests that her sensitivity fueled the normativity that eventually secured her debilitation. Holiday was denied the civic privileges that her fame secured. In essence, her melancholy serviced and was structured by the melancholy of a burgeoning normative American nationhood. The year was 1959, and Holiday died from the trauma of both chemical and social withdrawal after receiving no special medical treatment under the name of "Mrs. Eleanor McKay." "She was just another poor, colored junkie woman. They put her on a cot, parked her in the hallway, and went about their business" (*Lady Day,* 184). Ultimately, the blueswoman's redress proved to be no match for America's culture of melancholy during the Depression.

2 RECONSTITUTED MELANCHOLY

Impossible Mourning and the Prevalence
of Ritual and Race in August Wilson's
The Piano Lesson

In *Defending the Spirit*, Randall Robinson raises a critical question:

> From slavery we have sublimated our feelings about white people. We
> have fought for our rights while hiding our feelings toward whites who
> tenaciously denied us those rights. We have even, I suspect, hidden those
> feelings from ourselves. It is how we have survived. Black folk of my time
> talk about white people and their predilections at least once daily. But
> never talk about or with anger. It seems unnatural. Where have we stored
> the pain and at what price? (4)

Robinson, one of the most respected voices of critical race consciousness
during the 1990s, identifies psychic blockage at the intersection of African
America's history of racial subjugation and the community's resistance and
healing. Robison clearly suggests a need for collective mourning. Moreover,
he suggests that this unfinished grief work is grounded in the social body's
will to survive. Robinson provides a compelling invitation to explore more
critically the price of disavowed history and its devices. In what follows, I
take up Robinson's critical invitation by exploring Wilson's rendering of the
legacy of African America's disremembered past under racial slavery and
subjugation in *The Piano Lesson* (1990).

Wilson is perhaps best known for his use of drama to raise consciousness,
refusing to see the action of drama as a realm separate from the influences of
a participating audience and vice versa. For that reason, this chapter insists
that the import of Wilson's play resides in this reciprocity. Indeed, Wilson's
goal throughout his ten-play cycle was to lead theatergoers toward "a sense
of self-worth by identifying one's past."[1] The descendant of a German im-

migrant and a black sharecropper, Wilson's creative sensibilities developed out of personal and social conflict. Recounting his social history, Wilson "divulged that his parents concealed the wrongs and indignities they suffered in their early years. He characterized their deliberate cover-up as a means of shielding their six unsuspecting children" (Snodgrass, *August Wilson*, 215). Wilson found this position disturbing, noting "the fact of slavery is something that blacks do not teach their kids—they do not tell their kids that at one time we were slaves. That is the most crucial and central thing to our presence here in America. It's nothing to be ashamed of. Why is it, after spending hundreds of years in bondage, that blacks in America do not once a year get together and celebrate the Emancipation and remind ourselves of our history?" (quoted in Savran, *In Their Own Words*, 295–96). How do we account for the complexities of the psychical and cultural remains of a people forced to heal emotional wounds while wearing fighting gloves?

Wilson's play aligns nicely with the psychoanalytic critical tradition that includes Claudia Tate's *Psychoanalysis and Black Novels* (1998), Anne Cheng's *The Melancholy of Race* (2000), and David Eng's *Racial Castration* (2001). These critics agree that psychoanalytic criticism is indispensible for understanding the complexities of post-Emancipation African America's unclaimed cultural inheritance. In *The Melancholy of Race*, Cheng theorizes national and racial identifications as fragile, melancholic edifices—social formations and subject formations constructed and imaginatively supported through a dynamic of loss and compensation by which losses of self are disavowed and retained. Here, a melancholic social-formation is forged through the systematic exclusion of a racial Other, a racialization predicated on the false notion that differences in character and ability between the races are constituted within biological polarity. According to Cheng, the racialized subject stands as an object of national melancholy and a subject of racial melancholy—an identification built and maintained on social loss. As a result, racial melancholia for the African American subject formation is also a socially determined and unstable interdiction (Eng and Han, "Dialogue on Racial Melancholia," 345). Wilson's depiction of the northern extension of the Charles family line calls to mind the ambivalence of Anne Cheng's "ultra-sophisticated, and more lethal, melancholic" (105), subject formations that are at once objects of national melancholy and subjects of racial melancholy. While Cheng merely implies that it is the African American subject formation's ongoing history of social exclusion that keeps him or her suspended within the boundary between mourning and melancholia, knowing and not knowing the object or ideal is lost, Wilson makes the link between the Charles clan's impossible mourning and the lived experience of racial oppression an obvious one.[2]

August Wilson's *The Piano Lesson* is a unique meditation on the lasting influence of racial structures and events from the past on the lives of post-Emancipation African Americans. This paradox of the notion of "African American modernity" is no mere trope in *The Piano Lesson*; Wilson uses it as a paradigm for understanding how melancholy travels and reconstitutes itself through time and social space by way of the process of subject formation and ritual practice. The play lays bare a cultural melancholy, showing how melancholy is transferred and transformed as a result of and in resistance to an enduring struggle with racial oppression. In doing so, it critically reframes the process of racialized subject formation in terms of ritual, unmourned social loss, and hidden affect. As a result, the play provides a rendering of the racialized subject formation as simultaneously individualistic and inter-personal, providing a prism for situating racial identity as "one" constituted through "the many" yet unique from "the many."

In *The Piano Lesson*, Wilson stages parallel trajectories of psychological restriction sustained by post-Emancipation black men and women through ritual practice as they struggle for inclusion in a segregationist society that has historically subjugated them. Aiming both to illuminate and to historicize African America's gendered legacy of unresolved racial grievances, *The Piano Lesson* cites the fragile intimate relations and authority of white heteropatri-archal domesticity as its foundational, structural, and affective determinant. Moving back and forth between the Pittsburgh home of Doaker Charles in 1936 and race relations on the antebellum plantation of Robert Sutter in rural Mississippi during the mid-1800s, the play seethes with divides between the past and present that do not hold up. This haunting of the present by the past finds complication in the distinctly gendered desires of Berniece and Boy Willie Charles.

Avoiding the creative constraints of the linear narrative, Wilson's play offers an analytical address to the critical tendency to link melancholy and single-subject pathology, speculating about the transgenerational effect of unmourned social loss.[3] Thus, the play appeals to the antiessentialist cast of mind, offering a view of racial identity as a social and historically circum-scribed psychic interdiction that works though ritual, unmourned social loss, and hidden affect to discretely play itself out on gendered terms.

Race: A Socially and Historically Grounded Impossible Mourning

Between 1982 and 2005, Wilson wrote and published ten plays and earned two Pulitzer Prizes and a Tony.[4] Wilson's contribution to the landscape of twentieth-century African American drama is unprecedented and highly valued, with one critic remarking that he is "the preeminent American playwright of our current technological age" (Elam, "The Dialectics of August Wilson's *The Piano Lesson*," 361). On the other end of the critical spectrum, the dramatization of what Robert Brustein, in "On Cultural Power," has called decades of "black martyrdom" (31) is also commonly associated with Wilson's ten-play cycle. *The Piano Lesson* however, turns an analytical and constructive eye back onto the accumulative and unconscious effects of this legacy of racial subjugation. A thematic sequel to *Joe Turner's Come and Gone* (1984), the play recapitulates characters who, to borrow the words of Sharon Patricia Holland, "continue to occupy the same space in the country's racial imagination" (*Raising the Dead*, 15) as their enslaved ancestors and thus inherit the unclaimed psychical baggage of their forbears. Indeed, the play suggests that it is African America's ongoing experience of racial oppression that allows the past to maintain unreciprocated claims on the social body.

Wilson's Pulitzer Prize-winning drama opens in the Pittsburgh home of Doaker Charles in 1936. Doaker heads the household of a family struggling to overcome its ancestors' legacy of bondage and subjugation at the hands of Robert Sutter and his family. The Sutters, rural Mississippians, owned the Charles family during the mid-1800s. The stage directions preface the play's interest in racial slavery's unacknowledged claims on the Charles family: "The lights come up on the Charles household. It is five o'clock in the morning. The dawn is beginning to announce itself, but there is something in the air that belongs to the night. A stillness that is portent, a gathering, a coming together of something akin to a storm" (*The Piano Lesson*, 1). The image of a night that lingers before dawn is consistent with the theatergoer's schema. However, there is something far more nuanced to Wilson's staging of the play's action than a mere transition from night to day, for the imagery here issues a warning, suggesting a conflict between past and present that gives way to "something akin to a storm" (1).

Lacking the warmth and spiritual sustenance that characterizes the southern, agrarian way of life, Doaker's home is sparsely furnished and reflects the despair that plagued African Americans who left the collective experiences and relationships that nourished their struggle for equality in the south. Thirty-five-year-old Berniece Charles and her eleven-year-old daughter Maretha, the niece and grand-niece of Doaker, now live with their uncle and the empty promises of the Emancipation Proclamation. Doaker, Berniece, and Maretha represent countless African Americans standing, without roots, on shaky social ground at a time when the Great Migration was gaining momentum. Cornel West captures the inconsistencies of African American modernity:

The paradox of Afro-American history is that the Afro-American fully enter[s] the modern world precisely when the postmodern period commences; that Afro-Americans gain a foothold in the industrial order just as the postindustrial order begins, and that Afro-Americans procure skills, values and mores efficacious for survival and sustenance in modernity as the decline of modernity sets in, deepens and yearns to give birth to a new era and epoch. ("Race and Modernity," 69)

West charts the trajectory of a post-Emancipation African America that cannot ground itself in American citizenship and the progress it promises. Correspondingly, Doaker heads a household by working as a cook on a train and embodies West's modern African American of limited mobility. The family is stable economically, yet largely devoid of the skills, resources, and opportunities necessary to compete in the free world.

Doaker is one of two living members of the Charles clan who is fully aware of the story of how the piano connects the Sutter and the Charles families. The play's structure, spotted with Doaker's flashbacks, troubles the divide between north and south, present and past, moving back and forth across the Mason-Dixon Line and history. The play shifts in and out of Doaker's narrative of buried social memory. Doaker's recollections of the Charles family history serve as the conduits through which the past disrupts the real time of the text, providing the theatergoer with insight into the social and historical determinants of the melancholy that claims the Charles family.

In one of Doaker's retrospective monologues, the audience learns that the upright piano that sits in the corner of the parlor traces the Charles clan's progression up from slavery into the Great Depression. Originally, the heirloom was the property of slave-holding Robert Sutter, who traded Doaker's grandmother and father for the piano, which he gave to his wife Ophelia for their anniversary. To console himself and Ophelia, Doaker's grandfather, Papa Willie Boy, carved a montage of events, circumstances, and faces in memory of his wife, his nine-year-old son, and the entire Charles clan on the mahogany piano. The piano details the Charleses' social history of removal, marriage, birth, and death. On Independence Day, 1911, the grandsons of Willie Boy—Doaker, Boy Charles, and Wining Boy—sought to reclaim the Charles clan's social history of indignity by stealing the piano and returning it across the Sunflower County line. The theft gave rise to arson and five murders. Sutter accused Boy Charles, the father of Boy Willie and Berniece, for the theft. Shortly thereafter, Boy Charles was immolated in a burning boxcar of the Yazoo Delta railroad. Standing as a symbol of the family's bondage and struggle for wholeness, the piano sits in Doaker's parlor, holding the extended Charles family hostage discreetly. This post-Emancipation African American bondage is personified in the form of a spirit aptly named "Sutter's ghost," a specter that haunts the living members of the Charles family in a manner that connects them emotionally to their social history of bondage and exploitation.

The last standing members of the Charles family seem to be caught in a kind of chamber of melancholic flux that binds them unwittingly to their familial social history of social loss. Sutter's ghost figures as the text's metaphor for the psychosocial remains of the Charles family's social history of loss, dispossession, and struggle. The spirit strangely demands and defies symbolization, representing psychical and social conditions barred from the conscious recognition it seeks. Flashing in and out of recognition, the spirit of Sutter transitions between presence and absence as the Charles clan jostles between possible and impossible mourning.

Sutter's ghost is one of the most ambiguous figures in Wilson's ten-play cycle precisely because it inhabits *The Piano Lesson* in accordance with Derrida's logic of the specter. Derrida's specter is the "Thing" that looks at us and sees us not see it even when it is there: "it inhabits without residing" ("Specters of Marx," 18). The ghost is, according to Derrida, "out of time" because "one cannot control its coming and going because it begins by coming back" (11). The domain of the specter, according to Derrida, forms the tumult-ridden home of past and present, conscious and unconscious, and marks the grounds where ghosts of unresolved grief exercise their ubiquity. Haunting the play's real time, the ghost does not fit neatly either in the world of the living or the world of the dead but seems to straddle both realms. The extended Charles family cannot control its "coming and going" because the figure is "out of time," exempt from chronology. The spirit's ability to haunt those who did not experience the atrocities and terror of racial slavery is grounded in its capacity to be everywhere, yet nowhere at the same time.

The ongoing presence yet absence of Sutter's ghost results from the inability of the living members of the Charles family to circumvent the present-day triggers of the claims of the past on their lives. The ghost of Sutter is a metaphor for a socially constructed transgenerational haunting.[5] While the Charleses' post-Emancipation racial oppression is distinct from the racial oppression suffered by their enslaved ancestors, the psychical and material effects of the social conditions are haunted by this legacy; "haunted" accounts for psychical and material effects that do not directly result from circumstances of the past but bear the mark of a discrete inheritance from the past conditioned by the present.

The lives of Berniece and Boy Willie are laced with a general, everyday-use resistance that bears the traces of the real source of this transgenerational haunting. Though Berniece believes ghosts to be mere folk superstition, she also believes them to be walking around the house. For Boy Willie, the ghost transitions from the realm of mere myth to a physical force he literally battles. The inconsistent presence of the ghost of Sutter in the lives of Boy Willie and Berniece is symptomatic of what bell hooks refers to as the subjective impact of the constant "surveillance of white supremacy in the world of racial integration" (*Rock My Soul*,13). Boy Willie's retelling of the myth of the "Ghosts of the Yellow Dog" is laced with a narrative of ongoing racialization, ritualized resistance efforts, and haunting, the common denominator that links the Charles clan across decades.

In one of Boy Willie's retrospective monologues, readers learn about how Papa Boy Charles and four hobos were burned to death in a boxcar on the train called the Yellow Dog. According to the legend, the deaths were attributed to the vengeful hand of Sutter, who came home one day to discover the missing piano. Since that time, the Ghosts of the Yellow Dog were believed to be responsible for avenging the deaths of Papa Boy Charles, the four hobos, and other black men who died at the hands of white racial oppression. According to Boy Willie, the Ghosts of the Yellow Dog are responsible for a host of random deaths of whites of Sunflower County, Mississippi, who were guilty of crimes against black men. Boy Willie's recollection situates the Charleses' ongoing social history of racial oppression as the play's invisible yet central character. More specifically, coping with this ongoing social history of oppression forms the axis around which the spirit's ambivalent representative status spins and the Charles family bonds psychically.

The play's unique narrative of haunting provides an explanation for the widespread allegiance to the concept of race in the face of knowledge of its status as a social construct. Theatergoers are asked to go beyond sociohistorical and biological notions of race to consider how psychic forms and conditions render buried social memory and collective social history inseparable from racial identity. Indeed, the play suggests that racial identity is circumscribed by the ineffable nature of the social loss incurred through the interlocking trauma of historical and ongoing racial subjugation and supremacy. Sheldon George, for example, reads the allegiance African Americans feel toward the concept of race as a cover of protection against the traumatic effects of an unbearable social history:

> As this obligatory card, race is drawn, dragged, hauled, and conserved by
> African Americans as a mask that allows them to maintain but not confront

the trauma of slavery that lies beyond race's insistent return. . . . Racial identity becomes obligatory whenever a psychological link with the trauma of slavery exists for an individual. I argue that a link with this trauma exists to varied degrees of intensity for all individuals who identify themselves as African-American. ("Trauma," 62)

This explanation for the conservation of race is a sound one; but in insisting that racial identity is a politicized fantasy that results from rituals that shut the nightmare of social loss from racial trauma out of conscious recognition, *The Piano Lesson* grounds the conservation of race in the uncanny ability of cultural rituals to render mourning losses of self impossible because and in spite of ongoing racial oppression.[6] But where does this melancholy go and how does it work through ritual practice to link and maintain racial identities? In what follows, I aim to show how *The Piano Lesson* situates racial identity as an interpersonal psychic bond among individuals and across generations, bonds grounded in the ritualized reconstitution of melancholy.

Building on Freud's logic of melancholic ambivalence, Cheng helps explain why Berniece and the Charles clan cannot *keep company with* the ghost of Sutter and the role cultural rituals play in the racializing effects of these psychic injunctions. In "Mourning and Melancholia," Freud introduces the concept of the ego as the unconscious agent through which identification is produced and negotiated. Here, Freud locates melancholia as a psychic state in which the ego is ironically sustained by its own emptiness, filled to the brim with losses that cannot be known:

An object-choice, an attachment of the libido to a particular person, had at one time existed; then, owing to a real slight or disappointment coming from this lived person, the object-relationship was shattered. The result was not the normal one of a withdrawal of the libido from this object and a displacement of it on to a new one, but something different. . . . [T]he free libido . . . was withdrawn into the ego . . . to establish an identification of the ego with the abandoned object. . . . Thus the shadow of the object fell upon the ego. . . .

The ego wishes to incorporate this object into itself, and the method by which it would do so, in this oral or cannibalistic state, is by devouring it. (248–50)

The melancholic consumes the lost object it cannot know about.[7] Taking this observation a step further, Cheng suggests that the shadow of the object that falls on the ego is a metaphor for the loss of self that defies yet demands recognition. Thus, the melancholic "is stuck—almost choking on—the hateful and loved thing he or she just devoured" (*Melancholy of Race*, 9). For Cheng, melancholia provides a paradigm for viewing the constitution of the human ego—that is, the process of subject formation—as an ongoing process of legislating or feeding on loss. An overwhelming ambivalence plagues Freud's melancholic subject-formation. The melancholic is always already suspended within the boundary between mourning and melancholia, knowing and not knowing the object or ideal is lost. Sutter's ghost emerges to wed what can only be a temporary union between the family's egos and the losses of self they have inherited from their ancestors' social history and social present of death, inhumane bondage, humiliation, terror, familial disintegration, and emotional unavailability.

The specter's profound ambivalence makes it difficult for theatergoers to discern where the present starts and where the past ends. The audience has great difficulty policing the boundary between the lives of Boy Willie and Papa Boy Willie, Berniece, and Mama Ola. This ambiguity is clearly a vehicle for the play's theoretical agenda; *The Piano Lesson* moves in and out of flashbacks that invoke what Naomi Schor refers to as "the space of melancholy"—the "fluid, permeable, shifting" space that conflates the living and the dead, here and there" (*One Hundred Years of Melancholy*, 4). According to Mary Ellen Snodgrass, "Berniece's hostility suggests that the ghost that haunts the piano lives in her spirit" (August Wilson, 56). What is striking here is Snodgrass's depiction of the ghost as residing both within and beyond Berniece's psychic life. The ghost's haunting lays bare socially constructed and historically grounded bonds between the remaining members of the Charles family, those who did not experience the atrocities of racial slavery and their ancestors. Indeed, while both Berniece and Boy Willie are spiritually and psychologically imprisoned by the same hegemony that held their ancestors in bondage, Wilson urges the theatergoer to note that the subjective impact of this imprisonment manifests in the siblings on gendered terms. The remainder of this chapter will explore this perspective further, arguing that Wilson predicates these psychic claims on variable intersections of circumstance, unmourned social loss, hidden affect, and ritual.

The Gendered Legacy of Racial Slavery and Oppression

The thrust of *The Piano Lesson*'s commentary on the complicit relations between racial identity, ideology, and transgenerational haunting lies in its depiction of the gendered effects of enduring and unmourned racial injuries. According to Nicholas Abraham and Maria Torok, the buried speech of the parent "passes . . . from the parent's unconscious into the child's" (*The Shell and the Kernel,* 173). In "Notes on a Phantom," Abraham extends this logic, noting how "what haunts are not the dead, but the gaps left within us by the secrets of others" (287). The ungendering of slave communities during racial slavery had a lasting impact on post-Emancipation African American life. It is not without significance that Berniece refuses to play the piano out of respect for her mother's suffering over it. Boy Willie plans to sell the piano in order to at once gain economic freedom and pay homage to Papa Boy Willie. As the siblings battle with one another over the fate of the piano, Berniece and Boy Willie are claimed respectively by phantoms of their ancestor's matrilineal and patrilineal histories of racialization. Indeed, the perception and actions of Boy Willie and Berniece are distinctly constructed and mediated by their familial history under racial slavery. The unresolved pain of their ancestors uniquely claims the siblings. In other words, Wilson depicts the subject formation of Boy Willie and Berniece as processes along overlapping and divergent trajectories of transgenerational haunting.

The Piano Lesson's most compelling treatment of the gendered remains of unresolved racial grievances centers on the men of the Charles family. In *Ain't I a Woman: Black Women and Feminism,* bell hooks notes that because racial imperialism systematically excluded the black male from exercising the patriarchal rights that support the American social structure, "black men responded as if they were the sole representatives of the black race and therefore the sole victims of racist oppression. They saw themselves as the people who were being denied their freedom, and not black women" (101). One of Doaker's retrospective narratives reveals that Robert Sutter equated the worth of the piano with that of "one and a half niggers," the wife and son of Papa Boy Willie Charles. While Sutter took full advantage of his role as proprieter within the institution of slavery, Grandfather Boy Willie Charles attempted to avoid suffering the loss of social dignity that plagued its human chattel. Seeing himself and his father as men denied the inalienable rights of patriarchy granted by "nature," Papa Boy Charles's quest to steal the piano from Sutter is a gendered act of racial resistance. According to Doaker, "He [Papa Boy Charles] talking about taking it out of Sutter's house. Say it was the story of our whole family and as long as Sutter had it . . . he had us. Say we was still in slavery" (*The Piano Lesson,* 45). Papa Boy Charles's zealous desire to steal the piano is justified in language of proprietorship that reobjectifies an objectified community without recognition of the historical shame and emasculation that puppet the act in the first place.

Unemployed, selling watermelons, and unable to support and protect a family of his own, Boy Willie carries the torch of redemption for his patrilineal line. As Devon Boan explains, "No one seems to require psychological reconstruction through material means more than Boy Willie" ("Call-and-Response," 268). For Boy Willie, land ownership will unlock the door to social equality and bar his patrilineal record of indignity from recognition. "Boy Willie embarks on an archetypal quest for self-realization," Boan notes, "by attempting to purchase the very land that his family had been forced to work as slaves, and working it himself for his own profit" (268). Boy Willie explains to Berniece, "If my daddy had seen where he could have traded that piano in for some land of his own, it wouldn't be sitting up here now. He spent his whole life farming somebody else's land. I ain't gonna do that" (*The Piano Lesson,* 46). In resistance to Berniece's objection to selling the piano, Boy Willie explains, "Now, the kind of man my daddy was he would have understood that" (51). Boy Willie seeks to complete his forefathers' unfinished business by seizing the social and economic mobility they were denied. Boy Willie's counterclaim is one grounded in individual and collective loss. Boy Willie is compelled to wear and redeem the shoes of a collective emasculation. But Boy Willie is unaware of the fact that his quest for social and capital gain will serve only to paper over and enlarge the hole of familial emasculation and shame into which he has fallen.

Boy Willie's push to acquire land disavows losses of self conditioned by a personal and collective social history of racial oppression and black emasculation. Bound by the laws and social codes of Jim Crow seven decades after the Emancipation Proclamation, Boy Willie's will to "stand right up to the white man and talk about the price of cotton. . . . the weather, and anything else" situates him as the text's locus of turn-of-the-century-black-emasculation-turned-material-compensation (92). Accordingly, Doaker's determined nephew operates within an aggressive circuit of black-male-compensation that stems from the ungendering effects of racial slavery suffered by his great-grandfather, Papa Boy Willie.

Like his forefathers, Boy Willie still lives in the world where black male proprietorship, autonomy, and agency run counter to social order. Depicting the ghost's full fury when Boy Willie and Lymon attempt to move the piano with casters, Wilson warns against post-Emancipation African America's attempt to realize wholeness and healing through material means. Observations made by Wining Boy helps us grasp the thrust behind this warning: "How you know Sutter's brother ain't sold it already? You talking about selling the piano and the man's liable to sold the land two or three times" (36). Using his share of the $1,500 (the value of the piano) to buy into America's system of property and racialization only manages to secure expectation that covers irresolvable misery over systemic disenfranchisement. Indeed, Boy Willie's disavowed inability to compete in a game of property and commerce that secures profit discreetly through the racialization of space is a newly minted loss of self that finds cover in his relentless quest to redeem his familial history of racial exploitation and disenfranchisement.

Like that of Boy Willie, Berniece's relationship with the piano exemplifies how the disremembered secrets of her ancestors work through her gender identification to reconstitute themselves. As the matriarch of the Charles family, Berniece is bent on preserving the piano as the sole remains of her familial line. Berniece represents the countless African American women who fled the South during the Great Migration to become domestic workers in wealthy white homes in the North. For Berniece, the piano is priceless because it commemorates the lost lives and broken familial bonds that cannot be redeemed. But what Berniece may be unaware of is the fact that she is, like Boy Willie, a carrier of a unique strain of the Charles family's unresolved racial grief from unmourned social loss. Berniece's unwillingness to continue playing the piano after Mama Ola dies is a manifestation of a uniquely gendered family tie.

Berniece's decision to enshrine the piano as opposed to handing it over to Boy Willie's will is haunted by a troubled patriarchy fractured within and beyond the institution of slavery. Before the death of Mama Ola in 1928, Berniece was often asked to play the piano to warm her mother's "cold nights" and "empty bed" (52). Mama Ola's emotional availability declined at the loss of her husband to Sutter's wrath. In turn, Berniece's journey into becoming a subject began in the face of her mother's emotional unavailability. The piano's status as an untouchable object is Berniece's way of covering the pain of emotional abandonment by Mama Ola in familial honor and reverence. In a desperate attempt to circumvent Boy Willie's plans to trade the piano for money, she remembers, "Mama Ola polished this piano with her tears for seventeen years. She rubbed on it till her hands bled" (52). Protecting the tear- and blood-infused piano, Berniece vaults over "the gap," to borrow the words of Abraham and Torok, left within her by Mama Ola (*The Shell and the Kernel,* 171). The act of playing the piano, once used by Mama Ola to compensate for her unrequited desire for Boy Charles, now serves only to prevent Berniece from internalizing the lost mother-daughter bond the piano conditioned and signifies. Berniece's ritual of enshrinement allows the secrets of her mother's phantom to speak through the mouthpiece of her inability to live unencumbered by her familial social history.

By refusing to play the piano and move on to freely explore marital bliss with Avery, Berniece reconfigures the loss of self she inherits from Mama Ola by way of her own loss at the hands of white racial antagonism. Wilson couples Berniece's own "cold nights" furnished by the same white racial oppression that brought Mama Ola's Boy Charles to his death in a burning boxcar with her mother's loss and suffering to illuminate the social construction of this transgenerational haunting. Berniece's unwillingness to play the piano is the manifest content of her inability to mourn the loss of self she inherits from Mama Ola. Berniece and Boy Willie cannot exorcise the ghost of Sutter because it seeks to unite them with disavowed losses of self too potentially paralyzing to claim in their world of continued white racial antagonism. Moreover, all of this psychic restriction engenders the racialization of identity through familial and communal bonds and the rituals of redemption and resistance that consolidate them.

Impossible Mourning and the Prevalence of Ritual and Race

The play leaves the Charles clan caught in a vortex of impossible mourning, as the specter presents a "faultless" obstacle to Berniece and Boy Willie's attempt to move forward and define a self without mourning the losses of self they take on and appropriate from their forebears. Berniece's call for assistance while playing the piano, "Mama Ola, I want you to help me," underscores a correlation between rituals of cultural resistance and the reconstitution of melancholy (106). Berniece's call produces "a rustle of wind blowing across two continents," suggesting that her resistance is a crippled yet rooted effort that spans beyond the Middle Passage (106). After Berniece casts the spirit away, Wilson leaves readers with the sense that it still resides in the recesses of the family's shared consciousness and is scheduled to emerge again under the management of new circumstances. Boy Willie makes the point: "Hey Berniece . . . if you and Maretha don't keep playing on that piano . . . ain't no telling . . . me and Sutter both liable to be back" (108). While Boy Willie's request is made in jest, theatergoers are prompted to recognize the seriousness that lies just beneath the surface of his humor. The ultimatum Boy Willie issues prefaces a bond grounded in the continuation of the family's social history of racial resistance, impossible mourning, and reconstituted melancholy. By leaving readers with the impression that Sutter's ghost will return, Wilson ironically structures a dramatic conflict that does not offer resolution. Thus, it is a type of freeze-frame of melancholy that closes the story.

There is a profound point in leaving this conflict unresolved. Indeed, this very lack of closure is precisely what Wilson asks the audience to contemplate. The conflict *The Piano Lesson* stages yet fails to resolve invites readers to understand how ritual practices allow post-Emancipation African

Americans to repackage ancestral baggage *because and in spite of* the always already present threat of death, misfortune, and racialization. The simultaneity of the spirit's disappearance and Berniece's improvised performance reflects the rejection and retention of the inherited losses of self encrypted in her ego. If Berniece represents a melancholic subject capable of servicing her own psychic blockage in the name of resistance, it also follows that this ritualized impossible mourning is the domain of disguise for losses of self we inherit from others. How does one reject and retain that which refuses symbolization and banishment at once? This dynamic cannot be explained through the paradigms provided by Freud alone.

Nicholas Abraham and Maria Torok's theory of the crypt, an intrasubjective poetics of concealment, is relevant here. The spirit emerges from what Abraham and Torok might call the Charleses' psychic crypt of unresolved grief. The crypt, according to Abraham and Torok, does not contain the lost object; it entombs the "part of ourselves that we placed in what we lost" (*The Shell and the Kernel,* 127). Abraham and Torok's psychic crypt is a metaphor for the subject's ego, the holding pin for the "ego-ideal" or loss of self that is disavowed. This nonrepresentational loss reduces the ego to a "cemetery guard" (130). In sum, the crypt entombs a disavowed loss of self. The crypt contains a "loss that, if recognized as such, would effectively transform us" (127). As long as the walls of the crypt remain sealed, there is no melancholia. "It [the crypt] erupts when the walls are shaken, often as a result of the loss of some secondary love-object" (136). Abraham and Torok's faltering crypt enacts a wedding between the ego and its "ego-ideal," giving way to the psychic state of melancholia. According to Abraham and Torok, melancholia—a bout of strange and incomprehensible signs—is an unavoidable dynamic because the ego works overtime to guard itself from the incomprehensible loss of self entombed within and thus often fails at the task at hand. As the above formulation suggests, the emergence of the ghost's fury reflects the opening of a faulty psychic crypt of disavowed social loss.

Freud and Julia Kristeva furnish a critical nexus for understanding why and the racial end to which Berniece manages only to temporarily banish the ghost of Sutter through ritual. In "Beyond the Pleasure Principle," Freud locates traumatic neurosis at the limits of what he calls "sublimation " (7–18). Traumatic neurosis is the displeasure produced by the ego's inability to repress the loss of self that constitutes the ego (7). In contrast, sublimation brings satisfaction to the ego's encounter with unrepressed instincts and memories through appeals to the reality principle.[8] Freud's reality principle is the psychical injunction to conform to social codes in order to achieve the satisfaction of relief. The family's fear of Sutter's ghost serves as the empathic passage through which they appeal to the reality principle and access the emotional salvation it promises. For post-Emancipation African Americans, fear of white retaliation is a mode of survival, a means of satisfying the ego and forging racial community. Berniece's call for the assistance of her ancestors serves to connect her resistance effort to the collective suffering and resistance of her ancestors. Wilson positions the comfort of a unified community of resistance, which suppresses the fear of the real and imagined threat of racial oppression and terror, as the conduit through which unmourned social loss, represented in the form of Sutter's ghost, travels and evolves across time and space. In this way, melancholy morphs as it stabilizes a community transgenerationally.

Berniece manages to avoid the clutches of traumatic neurosis and land back into what can be read as an ongoing cycle of sublimation—a cycle of repudiation that uniquely works with and through the social body and its appeals to the reality principle. While acts of sublimation work through the pleasure principle vis-à-vis the approval of the reality principle to provide the ego with a veiled encounter with the unconscionable, traumatic neurosis is an unmediated encounter between the ego and a repressed event, instinct, or feeling. This meeting is fraught with the clamorous pain of trauma. In *Black Sun*, Julia Kristeva argues that the "melancholic hold" that temporarily secures the subject's primary identification must be maintained through sublimation—a dynamic that conflates and polarizes signs. Kristeva elaborates on this idea, noting that sublimation is a poetic form of melody, rhythm, and semantic polyvalence that strangely secures an *uncertain* [emphasis added], but adequate hold over the "Thing" (14). As Suzanne Langer reminds us,

> Everybody knows that language is a very poor medium for expressing our emotional nature. It merely names certain vaguely and crudely conceived states, but fails miserably in any attempt to convey the ever moving patterns, *the ambivalences and intricacies of inner experience*, the interplay of feelings with thoughts and impressions, memories and echoes of memories, transient fantasy, or its mere runic traces, all turned into nameless, emotional stuff. ("Discursive and Presentational Forms," 437, emphasis added).

Singing the names of Mama Berniece, Mama Ester, Papa Boy Charles, and Mama Ola, Berniece plays the piano using the rhythms of call and response, giving veiled yet new expression to the "nameless, emotional stuff" of her familial line. Berniece's improvised performance closes the crypt by reincarnating the unspeakable losses of self that have historically haunted her familial line, translating the language of the dead into a tongue more suitable for those who must live what Holland calls "a life-in-death" (*Raising the*

Dead, 18). Here, the "thing made ghostly" through generations of ongoing racial subjugation and exploitation remains barred from recognition and destined for reconstitution.

Instead of a resolved conflict, *The Piano Lesson* leaves theatergoers with the prevalence of ritual, signaling the ongoing, uneven, and contradictory impact of the racialized past on those who cannot live freely from hegemony and racialization. This melancholic haze binds racialized subject formations across time and social space through a host of ritualized responses to the lived and remembered threat of oppression. The following two chapters explore how the gendered and sexual dimensions of black subject formations stand as melancholic responses to the overwhelming force of impossible mourning wrought by rituals of resistance to white heteropatriarchal hegemony.

3 THE MELANCHOLY OF FAITH

Reading the Gendered and Sexual Politics
of Testifying in James Baldwin's *Go Tell It
on the Mountain* and *The Amen Corner*

When interviewed by Studs Terkel in the early 1960s about the writing of the semiautobiographical and bestselling novel *Go Tell It on the Mountain* (1953), James Baldwin noted how the blues informed its construction. According to him, "it was Bessie Smith, through her tone and her cadence" (quoted in Terkel, "An Interview with James Baldwin," 4), that gave him the key to the novel; for Baldwin, the blues is about knowing that "your losses are coming" (4). To know they are coming is the only possible insurance you have, a faint insurance that you will survive them" (4). Indeed, *Go Tell It on the Mountain* is concerned with how African Americans absorbed the shock of Reconstruction's ideological failings.

Go Tell It on the Mountain allows us to explore the sacred mechanisms through which internalized racism in the form of a stringent heteropatriarchy stands as the disavowed remains of the struggle for racial redemption in a white supremacist social order. More specifically, the present chapter examines the intense gender order that has historically framed the African American community's struggle within the context of the Pentecostal milieu that took shape in urban black life during the early twentieth century. All this, Baldwin suggests, happens at the expense of what he depicts as a bond between a blueswoman and what Judith Butler might call a boy with "gender trouble."[1]

A Blueswoman, the Pentecostal Milieu, and a Boy's Gender Trouble

In *Blues Legacies and Black Feminism*, Angela Y. Davis provides an initial entry point for this investigation by insisting that we read gender order into the condemnation of the blues as "the Devil's music" (9) in postslavery African American religious consciousness. "At the same time that male ministers were becoming a professional caste," Davis asserts, "women blues singers were performing as professional artists and attracting large audiences at revival-like gatherings. Gertrude 'Ma' Rainey and Bessie Smith . . . preached about sexual love, and in so doing they articulated a collective experience of freedom, giving voice to the most powerful evidence . . . that slavery no longer existed" (9). The blueswomen not only drew on traditionally sacred channels of communal relief and catharsis to attract a following but also outstripped the church's appeal in most cases.

The threat blueswomen posed to black national progress at the beginning of the twentieth century was couched in sacred terms but grounded deeply in a gender order conditioned by racialization. Baldwin makes the layers of disavowal palpable through the text's depiction of familial relations rife with gaps and evasions. Consider the closing scene set just beyond the Temple of the Fire Baptized, a storefront Pentecostal church on the poverty- and vice-stricken streets of Harlem during the Great Depression. Congregating after a late-night revival meeting, the novel's fourteen-year-old protagonist, John Grimes, and his family say goodbye to his aunt Florence: "Now they all stood on the corner, where his Aunt Florence had stopped to say goodbye. All the women talked together, while his father stood a little apart. His aunt and his mother kissed each other, as he had seen them do a hundred times, and then his aunt turned to look for them, and waved. They waved back, and she started slowly across the street, moving, he thought with wonder, like an old woman" (219). At this point in the narrative, John, who was once drawn to his aunt Florence's wayward sensibilities, no longer identifies with the image of a woman who has seemingly bent to the stick of his father's patriarchal authority. He must fall in step with the patriarchal order that permeates the secular and sacred black culture he once railed against. Indeed, John "lay changed under Heaven, exhausted and clean, and new" (215).

This view of John contrasts with the reader's introduction to a young man who, according to Baldwin himself, was "defined by things that have happened to other people, not him, not yet (quoted in Gresham, "James Baldwin Comes Home," 163). John's last words, "I'm ready. . . . I'm on my way," (221) is seemingly the beginning of his manhood in compensation for a historical legacy that prefigures his birth. His mother stands in the long shadows of the hall as his father polices his steps from behind. This concluding scene is out of sync with Baldwin's well-known indictment of black religious culture. Moreover, the scene is out of sync with the author's rejection of the enlightenment axiom that aligns heteropatriarchy with legitimacy and progress.

Nevertheless, Baldwin closes the text, leaving the protagonist under the influence of the sanctified power of black heteropatriarchy.

In my previous discussion of literary representations of blueswomen and normative American nationhood, post-Emancipation African American cultural integration did not do much to aid the social body's effort to achieve social equality. My analysis of *The Piano Lesson* illustrates how the shame of historical indignity was retained yet disavowed because and in spite of a marginalized community's perseverance and survival in a racist context manifests in gendered forms of racial pride and reverence. My analysis also locates ritual as one of the primary mechanisms through which disavowed social loss is transferred and reconstituted from person to person while fortifying racial community along the way. In *Go Tell It on the Mountain*, Baldwin exposes a route beyond the recycling of this inherited psychic baggage by exposing its workings and creating a context for mourning its attendant social losses.

John's transformation at the end of the novel can be read as Baldwin's fictionalized triumph against the heteropatriarchal norms couched in religious order. Indeed, *Go Tell It on the Mountain* has generated critical responses that overlook what may have conceivably been Baldwin's ability to mourn and recover social loss through its narrative representation. Farah Jasmine Griffin, for instance, claims that "John is now prepared to enter a new phase of his life—one that might eventually lead him away from the church. However, his involvement in the church provided him with the love and sustenance that is a necessary prerequisite to his moving on beyond the world of his father and to his resisting the tendencies of the larger white world to dehumanize him" ("Who Set You Flowin'?" 61). William Spurlin concurs with Griffin's latter point: "After his 'transformation' in church at the end of the novel, as John feels a wall come down between him and his father, Florence takes John in her arms and says, 'You fight the good fight, you hear? Don't you get weary, and don't you get scared. Because I know the Lord's done laid His hands on you'" ("Rethinking the Politics of Race, Gender, and Sexuality," 62).

Historical accounts of the novel's construction point to the sexual liberation that emerges from the potentially stifling effects of the Christian ethos. Pointing to the thin line between art and life, David Leeming casts Baldwin as the embodied artists: "John's night down at the cross is less the struggle for the soul of John Grimes than it is a metaphor for the struggle in the twenty-eight-year-old James Baldwin between the instinct that said, 'I have escaped my heritage; I can be free of it now,' and the instinct that told him he must journey to the very depth of the sorrow of his people before he could 'climb the mountain' and be free" (*James Baldwin,* 86). Taking Leeming's observation another step, we might read John's conversion experience as Baldwin's attempt to at once expose the gendered politics of the sacred mechanisms of racial redemption powered by the Pentecostal milieu and liberate himself from the stifling effects of heteropatriarchal hegemony.

When read in conversation with *The Amen Corner* (1954), Baldwin's dramatic sequel to the life of John Grimes, *Go Tell It on the Mountain* reveals itself as a text of and about testifying through which the author mourned losses secured by the Grimes family's faith and the white supremacist capitalist state at once. Published one year apart, *The Amen Corner* avows the interlocking gender and sexual effects of racialized people struggling to cope with the "object hood thrust upon them" on religious terms (Cheng, *Melancholy of Race*, 20). What are the effects of myriad losses of self secured by the racial oppression mobilized and motivated by the Pentecostal milieu? As opposed to confronting the myriad losses of self secured by racism, sexism, and classism during the interwar period's production of a white heteropatriarchal ideal sustained by the exclusion-yet-retention of racialized other, sanctified churches in Harlem New York provided a path cut around this grief work by promoting the belief that they were in the world but not of it. In essence, this cultural response to racial wounding is one of the many ways "racialized minorit[ies] [are] bound to melancholia" (Cheng, 19). Indeed, the mantra verified a present and future heaven separate from the relentless alienation and disenfranchisement faced by the saints "surviving grief" as they "embody it" (Cheng, 20). As Julia Kristeva reminds us, psychoanalysis would tell us that religion is "nothing less than an illusion," revealing more about the subject's false consciousness and illusory beliefs than reality itself (*In the Beginning Was Love*, 11). Baldwin's *Go Tell It on the Mountain* not only cracks the veneer of this illusion through its depiction of John's gender socialization as a melancholic response to the relentless trauma of white hegemony but also conceivably as a freeing of himself from the constraints of heteronormativity in the process.

The Melancholy of Faith

In *The Future of an Illusion*, published in 1927, Freud uncovers the status of religion as an illusion from a psychoanalytic perspective. This critique of faith builds on his interpretation of the origins of religious ritual in *Totem and Taboo*, published in 1912–13. Expanding on his explanation of the origins of totemism, in which he draws on the Oedipus complex to explain why the symbol of a deity protecting against human weakness initially took the shape of an animal to be replaced by a human one. The later idea of a human God is notable because it provided a more psychoanalytic context for a deeper understanding of the ambivalence that haunts religious idea and thought. If the child must replace the mother, his or her original source of protection, with the father, his or her original site of danger, then the child "fears him no less than it longs for him or admires him," an ambivalence deeply imprinted in every religion ("The Future of an Illusion," 699). For Freud, faith is the adult's response to the helplessness that plagues humanity. "This displacement of the oedipal conflict into a religious embrace of the Almighty can occur because religion has knowingly and subtly elaborated an account that makes room for and justifies" the belief in a God he at once fears and entrusts with his life (699).

Freud goes on to describe the symbiotic relationship between religious belief and the social crisis that attends the human condition. For Freud, religion "has contributed much toward the taming of asocial instincts" (699). Because religious dogma and practice provide the individual psyche enormous relief from human conflict—both intersubjective and intrasubjective—it tells us more about the subjective ambivalence that results from civilization's harness on the human condition than any verification that there is a God. Consequently, the psychoanalytic paradigm of melancholia presents a particularly apt framework for understanding the secular utility and longevity of faith-based religions. Faith-based religions may be said to sustain themselves through institutional processes that allow for the rejection and retention of a complex of unassimilable human frailties and capacities. Religious notions of "good" against "evil" find legitimacy in contexts rife with believers on their divine journeys amid "sinful" obstacles. In this way, faith works through myriad and ongoing human cycles of "fall and redemption" to naturalize its own authority. Faith is powered by the human frailties it constructs and naturalizes discreetly.

For this reason, the saints of Baldwin's Temple of the Fire Baptized have great difficulty being "in the world but not of the world." In this Pentecostal milieu grounded in racist and elitist societal norms, an absolute divide between the "sacred" and "secular" is always already susceptible to collapse. Readers come to understand what the saints of the Temple of the Fire Baptized could not see in their faith: Its propagation of white supremacist heteropatriarchal norms. Moreover, readers bear witness to an impossible mourning of social losses incurred by the Grimes family's social history of racial subjugation, which explains why this internalized racism goes untreated in the "house of the Lord."

Go Tell It on the Mountain depicts a community of believers who propagate the social exclusion from which they seek protection unwittingly. Baldwin suggests this recycled social exclusion and control is underwritten by unnamed racial pain and unmourned social loss. All this is kept in play as long as there are folks who are by default "in the world and of the world."

In the World and of the World

That Baldwin, during the Cold War era of the 1950s, chooses to set *Go Tell It on the Mountain* during the aberrant Harlem era of the 1920s and 1930s is significant.[2] During the 1920s and 1930s, the construction and maintenance of a white heteropatriarchal normative social base hinged on the racial other's association with nonheteronormative gender and sexual particularities. The body politics of the modern era, it is important to note, rendered the Pentecostal credo of "being in the world, but not of the world" an impossible feat for most saints caught in the nation's melancholic bind as what Cheng refers to as the "assimilated" yet "unassimilable" racial other (*Melancholy of Race*, 10). The belief that saints of the Holiness or Pentecostal movement could acheive salvation in the face of the body politics of modern racialization by faithful worship left such communities divided from within. This sense of doom and burden haunts John: "He had sinned. In spite of the saints, his mother and his father, the warnings he had heard from his earliest beginnings, he had sinned with his hands a sin that was hard to forgive. In the school lavatory, alone, thinking of the boys, older, bigger, braver, who made bets with each other as to whose urine could arch higher, he had watched in himself a transformation of which he would never dare to speak" (*Go Tell It on the Mountain*, 18–19). In a slump of unbearable grief, John is burdened by the weight of his unspeakable sin. Though John's homosexual desire for "older, bigger, braver," boys rails against social and religious norms, it was also a modernist era social truth.

Scholars of the Harlem Renaissance era note how challenges to heteronormativity were nurtured and contained in specific areas of New York City. Eric Garber points directly to the liberal sexual attitude urban blues culture promoted:

> They [the blues] told of loneliness, homesickness, and poverty, of love and good luck, and they provided a window into the difficult, often brutal, world of the New Negro immigrant. . . . [T]he casualness toward sexuality, so common in the blues, sometimes extend to homosexual behavior. In "Sissy Man Blues," a traditional tune recorded by numerous male singers over the years, the singer demanded "if you can't bring me a woman, bring me a sissy man." . . . The blues reflected a culture that accepted sexuality, including homosexual behavior and identities, as a natural part of life. ("Spectacle in Color," 320)

Like the twenty-eight-year-old Baldwin himself, John suffers in silent exile from the community of Pentecostal saints to which he belongs.[3]

This tight-knit yet unstable community is caught between the religious politics of racial uplift and respectability and a more liberal and influential subculture of Jazz Age Harlem. The politics of black respectability in a segregationist society, according to Horace L. Griffin, prompts black ministers and leaders to "present a restricted vision of sexual morality as possible only within the confines of marriage" (*Their Own Receive Them Not,* 19). Seeing the sanctity of marriage as a site of cultural reclamation, particularly amid socioeconomic forces that threaten its stability, positions the church as a battleground where the community's internalized racism is fought on economic and heteropatriarchal terms.

From Gabriel's religious, black nationalist perspective, his sister Esther's love of blues music is an offense to his quest to gain respectability in the eyes of the mainstream as a moral being. John's attraction to Florence's blues aesthetic provides a provocative image of a theological interception of his taboo identification:

> But John was staring at the door that held back the music; toward which, with an insistence at once furious and feeble, his hands were still outstretched. He looked questioningly, reproachfully, at his mother, who laughed, watching him, and said, "Johnny want to hear some more of that music. He like to started dancing when he was coming up the stairs."
>
> Gabriel laughed, and said, circling around Florence to look at John's face: "Got a man in the Bible, son, who liked music, too. He used to play on his harp before the king, you going to dance for the Lord one of these days?" (*Go Tell It on the Mountain,* 183)

Gabriel's rejection of Esther's blues aesthetic is significantly gendered. Moreover, when John recognized his homosexual attachments to "boys, older, bigger, braver," he was probably unaware of the gendered foundation of his desire. John is still immune to his father's gender socialization program and thus reifies a well-wrought identification at the intersection of deviant sexuality, femininity, and "sin": "Every Sunday morning, then, since John could remember, they had taken to the streets, the Grimes family on their way to church. Sinners along the avenue watched them—men still wearing their Saturday-night clothes, wrinkled and dusty now, muddy-eyed and muddy-faced; and women with harsh voices and tight, bright dresses, cigarettes between their fingers or held tightly in the corners of their mouths.... John and Roy, passing these men and women, looked at one another briefly, John embarrassed and Roy amused" (12). Ultimately, John identifies with this communal corruption and the ranks of womanhood therein.

John's embarrassment, like the shame of his Pentecostal community, goes unexamined and unreleased because and in spite of the abject poverty and marginalization that plagues Harlem. Though just as palpable and "invisible" as the "odor of dust and sweat" that hangs in the air of "his mother's living room" and the church (49), this affect must be ritually barred from thought. Behind the doors of the Temple of the Fire Baptized is where cultural embarrassment and shame quarrel with righteousness and fear, each pair fighting for the upper hand over the other and canceling one another and the community's recognition of its impossible cultural redemption from recognition. The remnants of this battle, Baldwin suggests, can be found in rituals that "burn out" the evil of feminine flesh (55). If the filth that permeates the Temple of the Fire Baptized cannot be cleaned and is gendered feminine, then the relentless attempt to clean what refuses to vanish suggests that the maintenance of gender order keeps the social loss that attends this history of racial subordination from knocking on the church door. As a result, John's obsession with cleanliness points to a kind of sacred passage around the unbearable forest of racial oppression and social loss paved by stepping-stones of gender order.

Significantly, in its resistance to white heteropatriarchal centrality and authority, patriarchal order's appeal to black communities was established and supported in part by the Christian belief in Eve's gender-determined fall from grace. That the women of the Holiness and Pentecostal movement are required to wear white, a uniform primed for filthiness, works to underscore their blind investment in the patriarchal order that renders them apt candidates for rituals of racial redemption. Moreover, the gendered politics of the community's impossible mourning gains its strength through patriarchal police, like Elisha, who desire Gabriel's "spotless" reputation. Collectively, they comprise a sacred web of impossible mourning that requires the ongoing indoctrination of apostles such as John to fortify itself.

This heteropatriarchy is stabilized until a gang war places Gabriel, Elizabeth, and Florence on bended knee, opening the floodgates of unmourned social loss the family has not come to terms with. When Elizabeth attributes Roy's unmanageability to Gabriel's lack of control, the observation is punctuated by an "awful pause" that prompts Gabriel to see the emasculated racial self that hides behind his self-righteousness (48). The ease with which Gabriel purges his discomfort by striking Elizabeth reflects her status as the most immediate site for displacing feelings of inadequacy. At this point in the novel, readers understand that the Grimeses' legacy of racial subordination leaves behind a pattern of unhealed psychic wounds cut and shaped into a sanctified tapestry of patriarchal order. Hence, the prayers of the saints, which arise out of the Grimeses' inability to cope with the social and psychical implication of Gabriel's inability to control Roy and keep his "house in order," function as interlocking rituals through which the family's social history of indignity and unmourned social loss moves across time and social space, taking up residence in John's psychic life. Baldwin lays the chapter entitled "The Prayers of the Saints" up against the chapter depicting the fate of John to allegorize the socially and historically constructed gender order that claims the novel's Pentecostal community.

Patriarchal Prayers of the Saints

The storefront church in the urban North is a place where Southern migrants have historically convened to transcend the psychic and social effects of the material limits of city life. Commenting upon Richard Wright's view of the paradox of African America's use of sacred discourse and rituals of the South to cope with the racism in the urban North, Farah Jasmine Griffin reminds us that "the church nurtures and sustains; it helps to maintain humanity and dignity and it ensures survival. However, there is no evidence that it provides the foundation for resistance to the social order. According to Wright, those churches which most retain a Southern style of worship offer the least possibility for resistance to the dominant social order" ("Who Set You Flowin'?" 80–81). In its provocative exploration behind the walls of the Pentecostal church where Southern migrants sought refuge during an era of intense urban racial strife and violence, *Go Tell It on the Mountain* provides another exemplary case study for a critical analysis of the ways in which racial melancholy is secured and reconstituted through the process of subject formation.

The three parts of this novel work in tandem to allegorize the socially and historically constructed heteropatriarchal order that claims the novel's Pentecostal community. The prayers of the saints arise out of the Grimeses' inability to cope with the family's failed patriarchy, a circumstance signified by Roy's knife wound. Testifying provides the Grimeses temporary refuge from the social loss they must disavow without haste. The prayers of the saints collectively lay bare not only a narrative of black male exaltation secured through black female atonement, but, moreover, allegorize John's heteropatriarchal conversion experience. "The Prayers of the Saints" divide Baldwin's depiction of John as the text's locus of deviant masculinity and his station as the prince of hegemonic masculinity.[4] The prayers of the saints collectively chart the sacred and silent (man)ufacturing of Baldwin's protagonist. Thus, Baldwin depicts testifying as the medium through which the Grimeses construct a heteropatriarchal cover for a reality they cannot recognize and embrace.

Plagued with guilt, the three saints feel they are all partly responsible for the hell that has brought the family low. As they take the opportunity to confess their personal sins in the name of familial atonement, we learn that their remorse takes the place of unrecognized losses of -self. We learn that Florence attributes the death of her mother to an unwillingness to adhere to the guidelines tethered to her gendered social station. Readers also learn how the emotional pain of her social loss brings her further away from the emotional stability required to resist relationships with those capable only of exacerbating her impossible mourning by introducing more pain and social loss into her life. An abusive relationship at its core, lustful sex with Frank is the medium through which Florence numbs the emotional pain that accompanied the absence of intimacy in her adolescent life. During prayer, Florence recalls the moment at which she is seduced by Frank's drunken touch: "She did not want his touch, and yet she did: she burned with longing and froze with rage" (*Go Tell It on the Mountain*, 87). The psychic and material effects of Florence's independent will are not strong enough to break the cycle of emotional bondage.

Like Florence's prayer, Elizabeth's prayer is inflected with the psychic and material effects of her familial history of racial oppression. Elizabeth's prayer seeks redemption from bearing a child out of wedlock. The stigma of her social transgression compounds the psychic wounding of Roy's battery. For Elizabeth, the words of her aunt, "you go walking around here with your nose in the air, the Lord's going to let you fall right on down to the bottom of the ground" (156), leave her feeling personally responsible for the racially motivated crime committed against Roy. If, as I have suggested earlier in my discussion, religious dogma and racial redemption gain their social and psychic traction in relation to one another and produce a gender hierarchy within Baldwin's Pentecostal community along the way, Elizabeth's prayer then reveals that her damnation can never come solely from "above." Rather, Elizabeth's guilt reflects the melancholic effect of a culture that uses women and all things linked to femininity as sacred tools for disavowing its loss of racial equality, equity, and well-being.

In contrast, Gabriel's prayer reflects not the search from atonement but reinforcement for his "anointed" status (94). There is no overbearing burden of proof or request for salvation here. Gabriel's prayer lays bare identification with heteropatriarchal authority made possible through his privileged male status. Unlike Florence and Elizabeth, Gabriel identifies with the sanctified image of maleness and power. While both Gabriel and Esther conceive a child out of wedlock, the latter bears the psychic burden of their social transgression. While Esther's pregnant body marks the material transgressions of two, Gabriel falls from grace and lands in the pulpit of redemption where he is washed holy.

Finally, it must be noted that Gabriel's recollection of his brief union with Deborah reflects and points to something beyond the gender order that grows out of the melancholic rejection and retention of a legacy of racial subordination that precedes and claims him. According to Trudier Harris, Deborah, raped at the hands of white men, unduly carries the indelible stain of personal liability for the community's history of racial indignity (*Black Women* 41). Deborah's willingness to wrap herself in the word, accept personal liability for her violation, and confine herself behind the Grimeses' door of domesticity acquits the community of allegations that suggest its failed patriarchy and racial inferiority. Indeed, as Harris points out, Gabriel ultimately capitalizes on Deborah's misfortune by marrying the community's fallen damsel and aggrandizing himself (*Black Women,* 41). Gabriel's prayer affirms his status as the community's beacon and purveyor of communal salvation. The religious strictures placed on Esther and Deborah mirror those that harness the actualization of Florence and Elizabeth; they constitute the four-legged platform of Gabriel's deity. The prayers of the saints show how the religious subjugation of women and exaltation of men stand in the disavowed name of racial redemption from normative American nationhood's aggressive denial of black patriarchy.

A House in Order

In *Black Sun*, Kristeva describes melancholy as a psychic state in which the modern subject longs for a time of purpose, a "presence of absolute meaning," that never really existed (171). Kristeva thus implies that melancholy serves as a compensatory psychic mechanism through which the trauma of the emptiness of (post)modern progress and, ultimately, social loss is kept at bay. Melancholy, Kristeva suggests, is the psychic state that blots out an impossible union with the unknowable. The melancholic's refusal to experience the unconscionable gives way to compensatory cultural engagements and performances. *Go Tell It on the Mountain* accounts for the rituals of everyday life used to cope with the psychical ambivalence that emerges from the tension between the African American community's search for salvation and the material effects of their socioeconomic disenfranchisement. With the Grimes family, testifying emerges as a means of "getting into Gods hand" in the name of escaping the "work of the devil."

Go Tell It on the Mountain provides a grammar for understanding why "women are more likely to be 'filled' with the Holy Ghost, more likely to go into trance, more likely to 'shout' and dance 'in the spirit,' and are more likely to 'fallout,' that is, fall on the floor in a spiritual faint" (Lawless, "The

Night I got the Holy Ghost," 4).[5] The gendered and formulaic codes that characterize these ritual scenes suggest that something more than the Holy Spirit and saints are in dialogue here. The intrusive and fleeting nature of these stirs suggests that they are underpinned by both psychical and social conditions that are at once inescapable and indifferent to the disruption they conjure and spread through the process of subject formation. Through the figure of John, we see how these rituals of cultural melancholy transmit and transform social loss across time and social space by way of the processes of subject formation and maintenance.

The "threshing floor" is where all that John's ancestors cannot acknowl-edge about their social history transforms into all that he cannot be. What is more, John's passage into the realm of hegemonic masculinity via his family's clamor for salvation situates heteropatriarchal order and faith as proxies for disavowed social loss. John walks though the fire into and through the image of his father, so as to keep the dead alive:

> He wanted to rise—a malicious, ironic voice insisted that he rise—and, at once, to leave this temple and go out into the world. . . . It was at this mo-ment, precisely, that he found he could not rise. . . . Only the ironic voice insisted yet once more that he rise from that filthy floor if he did not want to become like all the other niggers. . . . His father's face was black—like a sad, eternal night; yet in his father's face there burned a fire—a fire eternal in an eternal night. . . . A wind blew over him, saying: "Whosoever loveth and maketh a lie." . . . "Set thine house in order" said his father, "for thou shalt die and not live." . . . And then the ironic voice spoke again, saying: "Get up, John. Get, up, boy. Don't let him keep you here. You got everything your daddy got." . . . And as he turned, screaming, in the dust again, trying to escape his father's eyes, those eyes, that face, and all their faces, and the far-off yellow light, all departed from his vision as though he had gone blind. . . . Then John saw the Lord. (*Go Tell It on the Mountain*, 193–204)

The collective social loss of John's mother, father, and aunt does not arrive at the site of John's newfound identification with his father unadulterated. John walks a new path of identification paved by the hidden pain and social loss of his ancestors and directed by prescriptive norms of a more modern racial uplift project. Florence's descent into the subway after the congregation exits the church and enters a new day makes more legible John's path that rails against and subjugates all things feminine in the name of submerged racial shame. The image of Florence's social disintegration, signified by her descent into the subway, reveals her status as the familial medium of patriarchal and racial redemption.

The "holy kiss" Elisha plants on John's forehead can be read as a homo-social veneer that papers over prohibited homosexual attachments. John's homosocial dependence on the camaraderie of Elisha, his forbidden object of homosexual desire, illustrates the fragility of African American heteropatri-archy in a white supremacist world order. For John, this legacy of social loss and shame is not avowed in the name of "brotherly love" and aspiration: "I'm ready. . . . I'm coming. I'm on my way" (221). Needless to say, the Grimeses' journey home amid "gobs of spittle, the leavings of dogs . . . [and] the vomit of drunken men" (216) points to the fragility of all this hope and social pretense:

> [T]he houses were there, as they had been; the windows, like a thousand, blinded eyes, stared outward at the morning—at the morning that was the same for them as the mornings of John's innocence, and the morning of his birth. . . . And he was filled with a joy, a joy unspeakable, whose roots, though he would not trace them on this new day of his life, were nourished by the wellspring of a despair not yet discovered. The joy of the Lord is the strength of His people. Where joy was, there strength followed; where strength was, sorrow came—Forever? Forever and forever, said the arm of Elisha, heavy on his shoulder. (216–17)

The "sorrow" to which Baldwin's narrator refers is the unavoidable space where modern African Americans must visit but cannot rest. Indeed, the road of cultural progress and melancholy is one of ritualized resistance to myriad historical truths and realities. Pushed forward by the weight of Elisha, readers get the sense that John's identification with hegemonic masculinity will be just as ambivalent as the paradox of "joy" and "despair" that remain at war in Baldwin's Harlem community and the blues that serves as its mouthpiece.

Reading Baldwin's Literary Testifying

When placed in conversation with *The Amen Corner*, the writing of *Go Tell It on the Mountain* takes on performative dimensions for the writer himself. An intertextual reading leaves us with the question as follows: What happens to John's latent homosexual attachments beneath the pressure of an intersect-ing racial and gender melancholy in the context of the Pentecostal milieu? The mandates of black racial uplift and the church have always been linked. Moreover, *Go Tell It on the Mountain* a rigidly policed gender order is one of the effects of the politics of respectability that permeate racially oppressed and disenfranchised communities. Approaching the writing of Baldwin's texts with historicized attention to the mid-twentieth-century crisis of black progress and masculinity allows us to see how the works are engaged in disassociating both black homosexuality and homophobia from race—that is, facts of the black body—and linking them to the politics of racism and the cultural resistance to racism.

In both texts, Baldwin explores the relations between African America's religious social history, racism, the crisis of black masculinity, and black gay subjectivity. However, *The Amen Corner* is where Baldwin more clearly renders the avowal of black homosexual desire, its cultural masking, and black social progress within the context the Pentecostal church mutually constitutive. As he does so, he helps us understand the interlocking secular and sacred structures through which black homosexual desire is not only cloaked but also stimulated through this very masking. How did the prohibition against homosexuality of the first half of the twentieth century work through racial subjugation and the rigidly enforced politics of black respectability and gender order to socially construct black male homosexual attachments through its cultural cloaking?

A turn to queer theory might help us understand the unique cultural context that shaped Baldwin's treatment of this layered theme. In *The History of Sexuality: An Introduction*, vol. 1, Michel Foucault's "Repressive Hypothesis" questions the notion of a natural sexual identification and shows how categories of sexual identity—that is, the heterosexual and the homosexual—are socially constructed by-products of discursive practice (17–35). Foucault points to a hidden, complicit relationship between social forces and the thing (sex) they seek to control, suggesting that social forces bring into effect the very thing they seek to control. For Foucault, power reinforces itself by keeping this complicity/interdependency masked.

The Amen Corner asks us to think about how Foucault's "Repressive Hypothesis" holds up against other times and places. How does Baldwin's *The Amen Corner* anticipate and hold a cracked mirror to the surface of Foucault's theoretical perspective? More specifically, how does Baldwin's text, depicting an African American family struggling with racial and sexual difference during the Cold War era, collude with, resist, or complicate Foucault's theoretical perspective? The mechanics of the writing—that is, diction, syntax, punctuation, structure, author's voice, metaphor, imagery, meter, rhyme, etc.—in two key scenes from Baldwin's play is where we can find answers to these questions:

MARGARET: Where was you last night? You wasn't out to tarry service and don't nobody know what time you come in.

DAVID: I had to go—downtown. We—having exams next week in music school and—I was studying with some guys I go to school with.

MARGARET: Till way in the morning?

DAVID: Well—it's a pretty tough school.

MARGARET: I don't know why you couldn't have had them boys come up here to your house to study. Your friends is always welcome, David, you know that.

DAVID: Well, this guy's got a piano in his house—*it* was more convenient.

MARGARET: And what's wrong with that piano upstairs?

DAVID: Ma, *I can't practice on that piano*—

MARGARET: You can use that piano anytime you want—

DAVID: Well, I couldn't have used it last night!

(The Boxers and Sister Moore enter. David turns away) (*The Amen Corner*, 19–20, my emphasis)

It: what David Alexander cannot bring into view for public consumption or fully understand himself. The son of a black female pastor and an alcoholic blues musician, the community's aggressive politics of respectability renders David's homosexuality at once contested and enduring:

DAVID: A few months ago some guys come in the church and they heard me playing piano and they kept coming back all the time. Mama said it was the Holy Ghost drawing in. But it wasn't.

LUKE: It was *your piano*.

DAVID: Yes. And I didn't draw them in. They drew me out. They setting up a combo and they want me to come in with them. *That's when I stopped praying.* I really began to think about it hard. And, Daddy—things started happening inside me which hadn't ever happened before. It was terrible. It was wonderful. I started looking around this house, around this church—like I was seeing it for the first time. Daddy—that's when I stopped believing—*it* just went away. I got so I just hated going upstairs to that church. I hated coming home. I hated lying to Mama all the time—and—I know I had to do something—and that's how—I was scared, I didn't know what to do. I didn't know how to stay here and I didn't know how to go—and there wasn't anybody I could talk to—I couldn't do—nothing! Everytime I—even when I tried to make it with a girl—something kept saying, Maybe this is a sin. I hated it! (he is weeping.) I made Mama let me go to music school and I started studying. I got me a little part time job—you know? *I don't mean me*—I got a long way to go—but *it* gets better. And I was trying to find some way of preparing Mama's mind.

I got a long way to go—but it gets better (42–43, my emphasis).

David's "piano" no longer aligns with the piano he has historically played for his mother's congregation. Indeed, his actions and social position are never to sync again. A private and irrevocable exile is a place where this preacher's kid is locked. Such is the lot of black homosexuals constructed and cloaked by the politics of Black Nationalist respectability amid the rise of prohibited homosexual activity during the late 1950s.

Baldwin invites theatergoers to consider the more fluid sexual engagement among subjects who are socialized to question institutional power and authority. When psychic and social effects of African America's impossible mourning are filtered through and reinforced by the cultural prohibition against homosexuality and the heteropatriarchal politics of the black church, these social and psychic forces give way to and create an environment for the masking of the effects they seek to banish. *The Amen Corner* highlights how the aggressive politics and discourse of black respectability in the Pentecostal church create a cultural context in which what Judith Butler calls "gender melancholy" is subject to fragility and failure. According to Butler,

> Becoming a "man" within this logic requires repudiating femininity as a precondition for the heterosexualization of sexual desire and its fundamental ambivalence. If a man becomes heterosexual by repudiating the feminine, where could that repudiation live except in an identification which his heterosexual career seeks to deny? Indeed, the desire for the feminine is marked by the repudiation; he wants the woman he would never be. He wouldn't be caught dead being her; therefore he wants her. She is his repudiated identification [his melancholic object]. One of the most anxious aims of his desire will be to elaborate the difference between him and her, and he will seek to discover and install proof of that difference. ("Gender Melancholy," 137)

Here, Butler asserts that "normal" gender identification is a melancholic edifice accomplished through cross-gender desire and repudiations, gender and sexual identifications rooted in social loss. Within this symbolic system, the heterosexual male desires the woman he could never be. Inversely, the heterosexual female desires the man she could never be. Bearing in mind the power of ideology and its socialization strategies lies in the silence of their operations, Butler's paradigm helps us draw a profound conclusion about the relationship between discourse, racial melancholy, and gender melancholy: Within communities besieged by the paradox of national assimilation within the context of their social exclusion, the cultural life of racial melancholy can pose a great challenge to the gender melancholy of its members.

Since David cannot shake power's prohibiting gaze, he learns to mask his prohibited engagements. Baldwin's *The Amen Corner* lays bare the social and political underpinnings of men "on the down low"—that is, black and heterosexual identified black males who secretly engage in sex with other men. I read these sexually fluid subject formations as evidence of black heteropatriarchy's losing ideological battle with white heteropatriarchal authority and centrality. This loss is now legible to us in the cultural tendency to alienate and demonize gay and transgendered members of black communities; the increasing rates of HIV and AIDS among gay, lesbian, and heterosexual men and women in black communities; and the heterosexist epistemological agenda associated with the black studies project (on the grounds that it often disassociates issues of race and sexuality).

Ultimately, we might view the cultural impossibility and promotion of black gay desire as one of the paradoxes of the cultural reclamation projects advanced by segments of the African American community. By showing how same-sex black male desire is ironically conceived by heteropatriarchal anxieties and discourse that result from ongoing racialization, Baldwin's work writes queer black studies into black studies. At the same time, Baldwin's work writes black studies into the project of queer studies by casting racial and sexual difference as mutually constitutive dimensions of the process of subject formation within the broader context of the unconscious processes that attend racialization. Continuing in this vein of analysis, the next chapter explores how the cases of David and John are not the only means through which minority subjects living in a white supremacist society take up a life of ongoing, performative heterosexual failure.

4 QUEERING CELIE'S SAME-SEX DESIRE

Impossible Mourning, Trauma,
and Heterosexual Failure in
Alice Walker's *The Color Purple*

More critical work at the intersection of sexual and racial difference has been a theoretical necessity for both race studies and psychoanalysis for some time. There is a bias in African American studies for an analysis of black culture, history, life, and politics that privileges racial identity over other important categories of social difference, such as gender and sexuality. Dwight A. McBride blames the "the politics of black respectability" on the intellectual project's hesitance to explore the intersectional of sexuality and race (*Why I Hate Abercrombie and Fitch*, 43). The evolution of the psychoanalytic project from its privileging of sexual difference into a sustained analysis of the intersection of racial and sexual difference is also imperative. "Detractors of psychoanalytic theory have justifiably noted that, in its insistent privileging of sexuality as the ongoing principle of subjectivity and loss, psychoanalysis has had little to offer the story of race or the process of racialization" (Eng, *Racial Castration*, 4–5).

An interdisciplinary reading of Alice Walker's *The Color Purple* (1984) prompts the following questions: How might we reengage with psychoanalysis' privileging of sexual difference as the preordained and autonomous structuring principle of psychic life to consider its engagement with other categories of social difference, such as race and gender? Might it be remiss to forge a reading of Celie's same-sex desire outside the broader context of the normative and hegemonic white heteropatriarchal familial structure that circumscribes her social and psychical life? An investigation of the unconscious, psychical, and socioeconomic underpinnings of racial antagonism and its socially disorganizing effects calls for an analysis that synthesizes psychoanalytic, critical race, and queer methodologies. Through its depiction of same-sex desire between two African American women, *The Color Purple* provides an apt site for bridging the fissure that has historically estranged psychoanalysis and race studies.[1] At the same time, the novel disrupts what scholars have called a "white queer studies project" equally obsessed with disaggregating racial and sexual difference in critical discussions (Johnson and Henderson, "Introduction" to *Black Queer Studies,* 9).

Like Baldwin and Wilson's texts discussed in chapters 2 and 3, Walker's *The Color Purple* lays bare a slice of African America during the reign of American modernism. American and African American novels written during the modernist era, as Dorothy Stringer writes in her brilliant book *"Not Even Past,"* "do not often make testimonial appeals related to white-supremacist terrorism, racial poverty, or the imposition of Jim Crow" (89). Moreover, these texts do not often signify the impalpable, psychical forces that have unreciprocated claims on minority subject formations. Through an examination of African American subject formation at the intersection of racial, gender, and sexual difference, this chapter provides a focused critique of the disavowed inscriptions of white heteropatriarchal authority and centrality in black interwar life. Alice Walker's *The Color Purple* allows us to consider the complex process through which the racial and gender order that underpins white, heteropatriarchal authority and centrality work through the melancholic nature of the subject-formation to construct and maintain same-sex desire for those who cannot find refuge from the cultural politics of domination.

Walker, along with Fitzgerald, Holiday, Wilson, and Baldwin, represents the psychic effects of white supremacist terror in the form of an unassimilable void that is compensated for unwittingly on gendered and sexual terms. In doing so, Walker insists that cultural rituals and their symbolic economies of exchange keep the cover on this masquerade of melancholy. This masquerade, as José Muñoz explains in *Disidentifications,* does not always carry negative consequences, insisting that melancholia is an integral part of the everyday lives of people of color, lesbians, and gays who must do battle against oppressive forces. Muñoz shifts the focus of Freud's discussion on melancholia from a pathological force to a process of cultural resistance for people of color, lesbians, and gays. Muñoz poses a different understanding of melancholia as a "mechanism that helps [them] (re)construct identity and take [the] dead with them to the various battles they must wage in their names" (74). For Muñoz, melancholia—in its capacity to mobilize those suffering from abominable oppression and pain on the extreme margins of social order—provides a sense of agency.

The Color Purple confirms and presents an alternative to Muñoz's account of the generative properties of melancholia. Like classical blueswomen, Shug Avery ushers Celie through the haze of oppression toward healing and personal power without reincarnating white-supremacist logic and structures. In doing so, Walker's deceptively simple 1984 epistolary novel anticipates and extends contemporary theoretical scholarship on "deviant" sexuality. Forging a distinctively black feminist aesthetic through a rare depiction of same-sex black female desire, the text bridges the fissure that has historically estranged psychoanalysis and race studies. Moreover, the text reads the figure of the marginalized blueswoman through the lens of psychoanalytic insights to offer a new means of placing African American subject-formations in conversation with queer theoretical paradigms and perspectives.

Reading Black Subjectivity on the Margins of the Margins

Although *The Color Purple* has received much praise since its publication, the novel has been criticized for its "depiction of violent black men who physically and psychologically abuse their wives and children . . . [and for the] depiction of lesbianism" (Royster, "In Search of Our Fathers' Arms," 347–70). Indeed, the novel depicts Celie's journey of self-reclamation through a world of racial and gender oppression. Moreover, Walker also suggests clearly that the protagonist's recovery from the ravages of overlapping racial and gender oppression is achieved through female bonding. *The Color Purple* dramatizes these themes strikingly yet insists on a reading that does not confuse the novel's thematic and theoretical agendas. *The Color Purple* is not a novel about African American misogyny and black female lesbian desire as much as it is a celebration of the human capacity to make "a way out of no way" in the face of extreme adversity. Eve Sedgwick, in *Epistemology of the Closet*, insists that we must acknowledge the agency of the oppressed, noting that it would be remiss to overlook how "a variety of forms of oppression intertwine systematically with each other; and especially how the person who is disabled through one set of oppressions may by the same positioning be enabled through others" (32). Sedgwick asks us to consider how the trauma of racial and gender oppression might interact and overlap to give way to liberation on the axes of sexuality. *The Color Purple*, once criticized for being rife with characters who "do not seem to respond to [an] internal logic," invites readers to explore the undertheorized psychodynamics of social loss and compensation that animate the subject-formation at the intersection of multiple categories of social difference (Harris, "From Victimization," 9).

In introducing the social construction of Celie's same-sex desire against the backdrop of racial oppression and gender order, Walker highlights the difficult-to-trace role disavowed social loss plays in shaping and directing sexual orientation and desire. In *Aberrations in Black*, sociologist Roderick A. Ferguson introduces his "queer of color critique":

> queer of color analysis presumes that liberal ideology occludes the intersecting saliency of race, gender, sexuality, and class in forming social practices. Approaching ideologies of transparency as formations that have worked to conceal those intersections means that queer of color analysis has to debunk the idea that race, class, gender, and sexuality are discrete formations, apparently insulated from one another. As queer of color critique challenges ideologies of discreteness, it attempts to disturb the idea that racial and national formations are obviously disconnected. (4)

Indeed, while Ferguson's queer of color critique invites us to read the sexuality of racialized identities as effects of the demands of American state and capital; this paradigm misrecognizes, however, the interplay of the psychical and performative dimensions of the processes of subject formation and maintenance. This critical silence has much to do with America's history of discrimination through a compulsory dehumanization of the black body. Indeed, the nation's history of commodifying the black body as a form of chattel makes some critics of African American literature and culture hesitant to consider the immaterial dimensions of black subjectivity in pursuit of affirming the notion of a "real" living and breathing black subject. *The Color Purple* lends itself to a comprehensive understanding of black queer identities constructed and maintained by the performative properties of the process of subject formation and the unconscious workings of disavowed social loss and hidden affect therein.

The Color Purple's depiction of black female same-sex desire also provides a useful counterpoint to the tendency of feminist theorists who draw on psychoanalysis to situate sexual difference as "an autonomous sphere of relations" (Butler, *Bodies That Matter*, 167) to be considered in strict isolation from the influence of "other vectors of power" (167) and the propensity of feminist psychoanalytic theorists to ignore the impact of forces of domination on the psychic and social lives of black women (167). Walker, to use the words of David Eng, "asks us to consider how sexual and racial norms intersect to produce visible and recognizable subject positions and to consider how the homosexual and racial prohibitions that underpin the foundations of the symbolic order interdict a spectrum of repudiated social identities" (*Racial Castration*,141). According to Judith Butler, "it is no longer possible to make sexual difference prior to racial difference or, for that matter, to make them into fully separable axes of social regulation and power (*Bodies That Matter*, 182). Indeed, women of color are "multiply interpellated" at the intersection of overlapping social forms and conditions.[2] We also cannot lose sight of the fact that the repudiated social identities that bear the burden of either racial, class, or gender difference or some combination in symbolic order suffer compounded losses of self. This process is brilliantly illustrated through the character of Celie, a black, poor, and, according to general consensus, "ugly" woman.

Consider the following scene in which Celie's expression of sexual desire grows out of Shug's promise of protection:

> He beat me when you not here, I say.
> Who do, she say, Albert?
> Mr. _____, I say.
> I can't believe it, she say. She sit down on the bench
> next to me real hard, like she drop.
> What he beat you for? she ast.
> For being me and not you . . .
> I won't leave, she say,
> until I know Albert won't even think about beating you.
>   (*The Color Purple*, 79)

Shug's recognition of Celie's horrid tale is stalled, barred from consciousness until she sits to absorb its full weight. She is at once invited to see Celie's pain and her own privilege as mutually constitutive. Shug responds to Celie's call for relief out of personal responsibility, positioning herself as the cure for the ill for which she is to blame indirectly. What I find most paradigmatic about this passage is its depiction of the trigger for Celie's same-sex desire. Celie's desire for Shug develops from her inability to stand as a feminine object of masculine desire. Celie's same-sex desire does not follow the codes of "normal" heterosexual desire, primarily because she has not been affirmed by the prevailing standard of beauty.

It is not without significance that Celie's lived and remembered experience of sexual exploitation at the hands of the man she believed to be her father and Mr. _____ results from the fragility of African American patriarchy. Celie's biological father, a wealthy storeowner, is lynched by a mob of white storeowners who resent the economic and patriarchal competition. As a result, Celie's mother grows mentally ill and entrusts Celie and her sister, Nettie, to the guardianship of a stepfather, Alfonzo, who forces Celie to do "what [her] mammy wouldn't" (1). Under Alfonzo's control, Celie quickly finds herself the mother of two children who are taken from her arms at birth. Once Celie is "fixed," Alfonzo packages her with a cow and sells them both to Mr. _____ under the guise of matrimony (9). For Mr. _____, Celie's hand in marriage is nothing more than a hand of labor on a body upon which he performs "his business" (81).

The Color Purple exposes gender order as an extension of her community's drive to deny losses of self incurred at the hands of its social history and present of racial subordination. Celie sits at the bottom of America's hierarchy of social order and, in accordance with that status, services Mr. _____'s exercise of African American melancholic retention. To put this alternatively, Celie's status as a poor, black woman positions her as the edge upon which Albert redeems himself and his forefathers from their collective social history of emasculation. Here, "all that he cannot come to terms with about his lived and remembered social history of emasculation" translates into an odd mix of social limits and possibilities for Celie in the present. Consequently, Celie's push for sexual subjectivity grows out of the psychic limits she inherits from Mister. At once a black, poor, ugly, and infertile woman, Celie is valued at "nothing at all" in her racist, patriarchal context (219). Ironically, the patriarchal norms and ideals that govern Celie's subjection are the very tools through which she fashions her reincarnation.

In contrast with Celie's entanglement in the buried social memory of others and her own, the figure of Shug Avery is Walker's fictive meditation on the Freudian notion of polymorphous sexual desire, a human possibility most fully elaborated by Teresa de Lauretis in *The Practice of Love*. Reading lesbian desire in isolation from structures of identification, de Lauretis explains that lesbian desire is not overdetermined by any identification, particularly putting pressure on the notion that all desire is derived from the Freudian notion of "penis envy" (190). Instead, according to de Lauretis, female castration leaves girls bereaved of an ideal mother form. The loss of the mother's body gives way to trajectories of desire that do not emanate from the gender binary. By this means, de Lauretis uncovers a paradigm for desire that extends beyond what Freud imagined. De Lauretis's model ultimately allows for women to be subjects of desire that is more grounded in pluralism or, at most, intersections of identification.

In the film *Venus Boyz*, Gabrielle Baur provides us with models of lesbian desire that explain how one could desire sex with a man and a woman without regard for gender. Bridge Markland and other documentary subjects acknowledge their status as a "pansexuals." *Venus Boyz*'s opening scene features a performance by Bridge Markland in route to her performance. She characterizes herself as a bridge: "I am a chameleon; I am more of a bridge.

You can say that I am at home on the bridge. I live on the bridge. Interesting enough, the bridge is moving." For Bridge, she is a combination of both genders. By embodying the bookends of gender identification, Bridge manages to do much more than subvert sorrow or compensate for a singular loss of self. Bridge, with shaved head covered with a red wig, turns a transition from man to woman for the camera. We come to understand, through the catharsis that accompanies the drag kings' transitions back and forth across the gender divide, that the rifts in their egos give way to and are abridged by multiple forms of fetishism. Performances negotiated through an assortment of male genital prosthesis, wigs, makeup, and pinstriped suits mark the compensation for losses of self that indeed extend beyond those that might emanate from castration anxiety exclusively. These performances not only undermine notions of sexual desire that stream exclusively across the gender binary, but also mark its collapse in the face of circumscription through gender order. Indeed, the performances bend the discriminatory mind toward understanding the polymorphous nature of human desire.

Baur lays bare something de Lauretis and psychoanalytic and queer theorists misrecognize: Pansexuality is less a state of existence than a fleeting point of arrival or psychic achievement for all subjects who are not "properly" socialized by gender order. The ego of the pansexual does not adhere to the bifurcations that attend gender and sexual norms and, as a result, gives way to rituals that work through fetishism to channel and direct desire across the gender divide. We also come to understand through Storme Webber, another figure in the documentary, that not all lesbians work through cultural practice to maintain the melancholic incorporation of the social loss of normative gender and sexual codes that, if grieved, threaten "improper" gender socialization. The figure of Storme Webber reminds us not to lose sight of the fact that melancholic subject-formations who bear the burden of racial, class, and sexual difference amid normative social order find refuge in suffering disavowed losses of self. Storme Webber stands in for queers of color who, for some reason or another, cannot extricate and move beyond the melancholic incorporation of the loss of a feminine self she cannot embrace. Storme's uniquely nontransformative performance is consistent with what we learn about her gendered desires: She desires the woman in Dred Scott, another drag king Baur presents, she could never be.

Walker's Celie suffers from what is depicted as Storme Webber's arrested development outside the realm of polymorphous desire. What are the social conditions that circumvent Storme and Celie's ability to grieve the loss of a feminine self that secures their melancholic identifications with masculinity? Is it the trauma of the extreme abuse Celie suffers at the hands of Mr.

_____ and her stepfather that renders her incapable of releasing and working through the melancholic introjection of a feminine self that secures her identification with masculinity?

The stability of black female subjectivities that do not fit neatly into heteropatriarchy cannot be understood in isolation from compounded social loss disavowed and galvanized as such by trauma. At the same time, Walker's novel allows us to consider the interlocking social and psychical channels through which Celie's allegiance to same-sex desire is mobilized by the patriarchal gender codes locked strictly in place by racial order. *The Color Purple* ultimately exposes the chain of unresolved grief through which, for the racially oppressed, losses of self disavowed through racialization take shape in the form of things gendered and, by default, things sexual. The text chronicles the production of same-sex desire through the transformation of hidden affect and social loss across subject formations. This narrative logic of *The Color Purple* not only aligns with the queer notion that sexuality is socially constructed, but also shows how it is psychically and historically constructed by way of the fraternal twins of American modernity: racialization and impossible mourning.

A Way Out of No Way

Celie's desire for Shug is melancholic because it compensates for a fear-ridden past devoid of intimacy, both of which she cannot remember or forget. "It hurt me, you know," remarks a traumatized Celie, as she recounts her victimization (116). "I was just going on fourteen. I never even thought bout men having nothing down there so big. It scare me just to see it. And the way it poke itself and grow. . . . I start to cry too. I cry and cry and cry. Seem like it all come back to me laying there in Shug arms. . . . Don't cry, Celie, Shug say. Don't cry. She start kissing the water as it come down side my face" (116–17). Celie's testimony, rife with repetition and fractured thoughts, at once recounts the traumatic effects of the rape and bars the life of trust and intimacy lost during the event from awareness. As Cathy Caruth reminds us, a trauma narrative does not "simply represent the violence of a collision but also conveys the impact of its very incomprehensibility" (*Unclaimed Experience*, 6).[3] Put otherwise, because Celie is unable to come to terms with the self lost during the trauma of the abuse at the hands of her stepfather, all that remains legible is testimony that bears the trace of the traumatic effect of the event.

Readers encounter Celie's melancholic state of mind on the first page of the narrative where the protagonist strikes out the phrase "I am" and replaces it with "I have always been a good girl" (1). Celie's plea for the grace of a white God speaks to the racial ideology that conditions her gender and sexual oppression. Ultimately, she must "make a way out of no way," without beauty and, moreover, the ability to procreate. This process of liberation is ironically grounded in limitation.

The interwar and Depression era—marked by a decline in black fertility and obstacles to black family survival—witnessed a resurgence of organizations and agencies working on behalf of an African American domesticity threatened by racial oppression.[4] Celie's liberation is grounded ironically in her social limitations. That is primarily because Celie's life, like that of any member of a historically oppressed community, is a deviation from the norms in which it is rooted and policed against. Black feminist scholars, such as Evelynn Hammonds and Michele Wallace, note that oppressive material conditions that disrupted the application of patriarchy in black life pose challenges to psychoanalytic interpretations of African American cultural production. At the same time, African American life and culture, however deviant, "share a white patriarchal norm as a central point of reference" (Wallace, *Invisibility Blues*, 231).

In *Invisibility Blues*, Michele Wallace notes that what is at issue here for black domesticity "is not a moral or spiritual superiority by virtue of a greater oppression, or even a distinct 'cultural' difference, that allowed blacks to avoid the standard exposure to patriarchal power. Rather, material conditions delayed the application of the more sophisticated forms of patriarchy, and then continued to cause certain deviations or variations in their use" (230). The fight to maintain black patriarchal order in the world of racial segregation not only created a hostile environment for black female autonomy and industry but also placed a strain on traditional sexual relations in black households.[5] The 4,723 blacks lynched between 1882 and 1968, which were mostly male and often castrated, not only are the remains of a fragile racial, sexual, and economic order, but also spawned undisclosed deviant sexual relations behind the doors of African American domesticity.[6] Indeed, Celie's same-sex desire must be understood within the broader context of the normative and hegemonic white heteropatriarchal familial structure and racial antagonism that circumscribe her social and psychical life.

Celie's journey—that is, her way out of no way—is less one of self-recovery than a reconstitution of self. Celie's narrative does not commence at ground zero—struggling for subjectivity at the intersection of class, racial, and gender difference as a poor black woman—but, rather, begins at a negative space of "nothingness" where she hones a witnessing presence. Celie's reconstitution is more observational before it becomes performative. Before she is free to desire beyond the boundaries of the dualisms that bolster white heteropatriarchal authority, Celie desires within these social and psychical boundaries.

Celie's intimacy with Shug and sexual contest with Mister emerges from a psychical dynamic of loss and compensation. In contrast, Shug's unrestrained sexual expressions back and forth across the sex divide point to the fact that her sexual desire does not stem from a wellspring of psychic loss and compensation. The social and historical construction of Celie's same-sex desire is made legible as it develops through and against what Tim Dean might call Shug's impersonal desire.

In *Beyond Sexuality*, Dean introduces an "impersonalist conception of sexuality," arguing that sexual orientation—normative and deviant—is not biologically determined and has no value outside of language and culture (274). Drawing upon Jacques Lacan's theory of desire, Dean asserts that desire and fantasy involve an object and accordingly reveal "the origin of desire as nonheterosexual" (274). Dean makes the point:

> Lacan's theory of desire gives the lie to compulsory heterosexuality. It follows that if desire is, in the first instance, impersonal then our primary relations aren't with other persons. The human infant relates to its mother not as a person but as an object. We start to see that, harsh though it may sound to say so, other people provide merely contingent supports for psychical relations that are at the bottom impersonal. This being the case, the impersonalist conception of sexuality gives rise to different ideas about relationality. (274)

By highlighting the relational and constructed nature of sexual identifications and expressions, Dean questions the assumption that sexual attachments are unmediated and natural. Instead, Dean suggests that sexual attachments are conduits through which impersonal drives find expression.

Shug's polymorphous desire, consistent with her blueswoman status, is the text's locus of the unfettered human condition. As a black woman thrown from the ranks of a religious family, Shug's desire is explored from a location that cannot be embraced by those clamoring for inclusion in normative American nationhood. Shug's sexual desire emerges against the sanctioned logic of its production. The vein through which Shug creates and desires, affectionately termed "creation," exists beyond the limits of language and normative cultural construction. While Shug exceeds the gender and sexual binaries of normativity, the initial stage of Celie's journey is overdetermined by such dualism.

Dean's insight pairs nicely with Judith Butler's theory of normative sexual identification toward the task of illuminating the melancholic and gendered underpinnings of Celie's sexual attachment to Shug. In *The Psychic Life of Power,* Butler accounts for the subject's journey toward the construction of a heterosexual identification. Butler asserts that this process demands the disavowal of the loss of homosexual attachments. For Butler, "normal," heterosexual identification comes into being by way of what she calls "gender melancholy." Butler asserts that "normal" gender identification is a melancholic edifice accomplished through cross-gender desire and repudiations, gender and sexual identifications linked and rooted in disavowed social loss. Within this symbolic system, the heterosexual male desires the woman he could never be. Inversely, the heterosexual female desires the man she could never be. Butler's logic helps us understand lesbianism and homosexuality as sexual identifications stabilized through the interplay of "inappropriate" gender identifications and performances.

In *The Color Purple*, such deviance stands as the traumatic effect of racial order. Celie is a woman who desires and disclaims feminine identity because she is a lightning rod for black patriarchal anxieties. Celie's sexual pursuit of Shug works in the service of a compulsory masculinity enacted to bar the social losses of her feminine past from awareness. Celie's sexual desire for Shug is a vehicle of ongoing melancholic self-recovery, a perpetual sealing off of a traumatic wound that is unrelated to Shug and lesbianism. Celie's sexual desire for Shug is impersonal, a compensation for an unconscious loss of self. If Celie's same-sex desire works discretely in the service of barring her feminine past from awareness, then what, other than masculine gender identification, is her recognizable behavioral motivation?

Consider the following scene in which Celie appropriates the male gaze: "All the men got they eyes glued to Shug's bosom. I got my eyes glued there too. I feel my nipples harden under my dress. My little button sort of perk up too. Shug, I say to her in my mind, Girl, you looks like a real good time, the Good Lord knows you do" (*The Color Purple,* 85). Especially noteworthy here is the suggestion that Celie's attraction to Shug is a manifestation of masculine identification. Celie's fundamental dilemma throughout the novel is the need to exile the social losses of her feminine past to the recesses of her unconscious. Thus, we can see Celie's same-sex desire as not much more than a means to another, more material, end negotiated through individual and social performance. This dynamic is represented most clearly when readers find Celie nestling into a masculine identification as she looks at Shug's naked body: "First time I got the full sight of Shug Avery long black body with it black plum nipples, look like her mouth, I thought I had turned into a man" (52). Celie also takes advantage of the opportunity to bond with Albert, her primary oppressor, in the name of exercising the patriarchal right to protect Shug's virtue. Celie explains: "This is the closest us ever felt" (57). Ultimately, Celie's impersonal desire is directed by gender binary through which heterosexuality traffics.

Ironically, Celie's mode of compensation for the social loss she disavows is filtered through the same patriarchal codes of her condemnation. Celie seems to curb the pain of her feminine past by taking on the gender identity of her oppressors.[7] This is most evident when she gives Harpo advice on how to manage Sophia's disobedience: "I think bout how every time I jump when Mr. _____ call me, she look surprise. And like she pity me. . . . Beat her I say. . . . I say it cause I'm a fool, I say. I say it cause I'm jealous of you. I say it cause you do what I can't" (38–42). Celie forges an alliance of patriarchal dominance in the name of forging a counternarrative to the emotional destitution that threatens to condemn her spirit. In keeping with the fragile nature of melancholic identity formations, Celie's disavowal of social loss incurred through her abusive past is a continual, never completed, process.[8] We must not lose sight of the fact that Celie's gender melancholy is an insecure refuge from identification with "all things feminine" in her fight against black patriarchy's reclamation campaign. The entanglement and undoing of this bind is the crux of the novel's black feminist aesthetic. Indeed, Walker's novel of epistolary realism provides a prescription for the issue it diagnoses.

The Gendered and Sexual Remains of Untreated Racial Pain

Many poststructuralist critics have acknowledged that heterosexuality and homosexuality acquired their mutually exclusive meanings under the sign of racial difference in the name of normalizing and guaranteeing the reproduction of a white heteropatriarchy.[9] And queer psychoanalytic critics have drawn on this claim in their own work, arguing that this mutually constitutive crossing of sexual and racial difference is integral to our contemporary sense of self as modern liberal (sexualized as well as racialized) subjects.[10] In *Totem and Taboo*, Freud pairs the figure of the primitive and deviant sexual practices. Inversely, the figure of the homosexual in Freud's "On Narcissism" serves as a stand-in for racial difference. It is Eng's assertion in *Racial Castration* that subjectivity depends intimately on racializing and sexualizing strategies that are marked by both conscious and unconscious forces that I have aimed to build on here.

Perhaps no text so fully addresses the ubiquitous and persistent will of melancholy to travel across social pace through the process of subject formation as does *The Color Purple*. The idea that psychoanalysis is not equipped to forge its own analytical evolution is what *The Color Purple* opens to interrogation. Reading Walker's narrative through the lens of the concept of melancholia counteracts the tendency of critics of queer studies to ignore racial difference and racialization as they relate to sexual orientation and unconscious processes. Just as racial antagonism is not exempt from unconscious, psychical forces, neither is the subjective impact of these forces.

Celie's same-sex desire demands a reading that accounts for the role that racialization and its unconscious subjective life play in the formation and maintenance of her "improper" gender identification and sexual attachment. "When [Celie] hear[s] them [Albert and Shug] together all [she] can do is pull the quilt over [her] head and finger [her] little button and titties and cry" (*The Color Purple*, 83). Celie's tears at once trace her same-sex desire to her unconscionable past as a feminine object of abuse and tie them to the socially disorganizing effects of racial order. Mr. _____'s oppressive behavior is an extension of the white supremacist terror Alfonzo channeled. Celie's masturbation can be read as ritual of melancholic retention. The protagonist's same-sex desire develops in response to two overlapping melancholic states, her own gender melancholy and Albert's racial melancholy.

Walker's take on black patriarchy, which is neither the black-emasculation-turned-material-compensation represented by Wilson's Boy Willie nor the religious mode of patriarchal redemption offered by Baldwin's Gabriel, offers the lowest common dominator in the figure of Mr. _____: domestic violence. Mr. _____ gives Harpo a lesson in African American patriarchal redemption: "Wives is like children. You have to let 'em know who got the upper hand. Nothing can do that better than a good sound beating" (37). No other figure in the African American literary canon seems to negotiate racial reclamation through misogynistic extremes more than Mr. _____. Conditioned by the laws and social codes of Jim Crow Georgia, Mr. _____'s lesson in African American patriarchal redemption is the by-product of generations of unredeemed black emasculation. Raped by the man she believes to be her father and battered by her husband, Celie bears the brunt of myriad losses of self incurred by her forefathers. Celie is the body upon which Mr. _____ practices his theory and the conduit through which he secures the reconstitution of his own social loss and its repacking in her same-sex desire.

A trace of this example of cultural melancholy can be found in one of Celie's trauma narratives. Let's return to this moment: "It scare me just to see it. And the way it poke itself and grow. . . . I start to cry too. I cry and cry and cry. Seem like it all come back to me laying there in Shug arms" (116–17).

Shug furnishes intimacy that provides Celie only a raincoat of protection from the encroaching storm of her disremembered past rather than complete shelter from its claims. My conclusion, in this regard, is, perhaps, finally a layered one: Once Celie draws on gender order to secure refuge from her past subjugation as a feminine body, her liberation hinges on a resolutely fragile masculine identification. For Celie, masculinity is a fragile point of arrival reified through performance rituals. In Celie's limited social context, Shug is the only partner available and willing to help her achieve liberation from her past of abuse. What matters most to Celie is not so much lesbian desire, but the expression of desire that yields masculine identification.

Significantly, it is through expressions of same-sex desire that Celie attempts to secure the illusion that her new, masculine reality was always there. The struggle Celie has with sewing in Shug's absence makes this dynamic quite evident. Through the sale of her gender-bending "folkpants," Celie follows the heterosexual codes of gender order and uses them to sustain her psychosocial recovery. The ritualized construction of folkpants not only allowed the seamstress to remain on her preferred side of the gender line but, moreover, forge a secure residence within the realm of masculinity. Celie recalls her folkpant-making frenzy: "I sit in the dining room making pants after pants. I got pants now in every color and size under the sun. Since us started making pants down home, I ain't been able to stop. I change the cloth, I change the print, I change the waist, I change the pocket. I change the hem, I change the fullness of the leg. I make so many pants Shug tease me. I didn't know what I was starting, she say, laughing" (218–19). Each stitch weakens Celie's identification with femininity and strengthens her identification with masculinity. "My life," Celie states, "stop when I left home, I think. But then I think again. It stop with Mr. _____ maybe, but start up again with Shug" (85). But just as Celie gets "on [her] feet" (218), she learns that Shug "gots the hots for a boy of nineteen" (255). Once Celie finds herself without Shug, her attempts to fortify her masculine identification through the construction of folkpants are rendered unproductive without the blues singer's visible, oppositional status: "I set here in the big house by myself trying to sew, but what good is sewing gon do? What good is anything? Being alive begin to seem like an awful strain" (262).

Celie eventually forges a homosocial bond with Albert to fill this absence. For Celie, Mr. _____ "aint Shug, but he begins to be somebody [she] can talk to" (283). Celie's bond with Mr. _____ is more platonic than oppositional, more intimate than antagonistic. Significantly, Celie and Mr. _____'s rekindled relationship begins to take melancholic precedence over any sexual desire for Shug. The relationship serves to affirm and fortify her masculine identification of disavowed social loss. Bonding with Mr. _____ forms a ritual of melancholic retention that allows Celie to keep the Lacanian real in perpetual obfuscation. In keeping with the principles of womanism, Celie makes "a way out of no way" in the service of survival and wholeness. Celie's permanent banishment from and flawed appropriation of the heteropatriarchal norm can be used as a model for a psychically, materially, and racially contingent theory of female same-sex desire. Walker's narrative situates the disavowed social loss—that is, the American myth of cross-class white racial sameness, purity, and promise—that underpins the ritualized normalization of the white, heteropatriarchal centrality and authority as the recycled psychic substrate through which minority female same-sex desire is produced and determined.

Acknowledging the socially disorganizing effect of racial order, Evelynn Hammonds has suggested that theorizing about and through black lesbian sexuality requires one to consider the forces of repression and domination experienced by black women in general.[11] I have argued throughout this chapter that theorizing black female same-sex desire requires a grammar for understanding how social loss is disavowed and compensated for through expressions of desire informed distinctly by the subject's relationship to racial and patriarchal order and trauma. My observations of the disavowed social loss that mobilized Celie's same-sex desire across subject-formations through the process of subject formation is one of countless untold stories of survival in American nationhood's field of cultural melancholy. Walker's complex depiction of black female same-sex desire provides a useful paradigm for understanding and building on the unconscious mechanisms, the "pull" of disavowed social loss and compensation, that animate subjects of historical and present-day racial antagonism within the context of other categories of social difference. Indeed, when plotted in the nation's field of cultural melancholy, we see how Celie's "deviant" desire is overdetermined by circumstances past and present and, as such, will remain unstable and primed for transformation.

5 A CLEARING BEYOND THE MELANCHOLIC HAZE

Staging Racial Grieving in
Suzan-Lori Parks's *Venus* and
Tony Kushner's *Caroline, or Change*

How do a people go about living freely after a social history of experiences and circumstances that negate the concept of a free, autonomous self? Much of contemporary African American literature is concerned with the ongoing and ritualized work of negotiating racial identification within the context of a traumatic past and present. For instance, Sethe, the protagonist of Toni Morrison's *Beloved* (1987), struggles to claim a self entangled with a history of social indignity that cannot be shaken after she murders and frees her child from the bondage of slavery. "She was my best thing" (275), Sethe explains to her companion Paul D. Paul D retorts, "You your best thing, Sethe. You are" (275). Paul D points to identification possibilities to which Sethe has lost access. Not unlike the post-Emancipation characters that populate Morrison's novel, Sethe forgoes grieving this loss of self in favor of avoiding deep-seated despair. The community's exorcism that banishes the figure of Beloved—Morrison's fictional representation of the myriad social losses incurred under the history of racial slavery—is designed to provide psychic relief and communal stability by sealing off portions of the past from the present. Unruly, the hidden affect and the loss of self it encrypts take on a disavowed life of their own, directing the thoughts and actions of others clandestinely:

> So they forgot her. Like an unpleasant dream during a troubling sleep. Occasionally, however, the rustle of a skirt hushes when they wake, and the knuckles brushing a cheek in sleep seem to belong to the sleeper. Sometimes the photograph of a close friend or relative—looked at too long—shifts, and something more familiar than the dear face itself moves

there. They can touch it if they like, but don't, because they know things
will never be the same if they do. (275)

Things will never be the same if they touch it. For the members of Morrison's post-Emancipation African American community, their union in
melancholy, however dysfunctional, must take precedence over the work
of grief. Since, as Anne Cheng reminds us, the melancholia African Americans suffer is inextricably linked to authority's melancholic attachments
to dominant ideals, might racial grief work provide the only empathic
passage to community and equity across racial lines?[1] What does it mean
that in *Beloved* racial melancholy's persistence is grounded in communal
formation and resistance? If racial melancholy persists as a consequence
of the ritualized consolidation of racial identifications and communities,
might communal practice that denaturalizes racial identification move us
beyond this melancholic haze? How have contemporary playwrights ad-
dressed these issues?

Impossible mourning underlies the thematic concerns of much of contemporary American drama. Imagining a life beyond the grips of racial melancholy for the protagonists in Suzan-Lori Parks's *Venus* (1996) and Tony
Kushner's *Caroline, or Change* (2004) is both compelling and difficult. It is
compelling because Parks's Venus and Kushner's Caroline are clearly controlled by the unreciprocated claims of lost and unmourned identification
possibilities. It is difficult because these unreciprocated and harmful claims
are symptomatic of the subjects' struggles for psychic survival in a nation
that builds and maintains the melancholic edifice we know as "normativity"
through the ritualized exclusion of black and nonnormative subjects.[2] My
brief discussion of Morrison's *Beloved* attributes the onset and maintenance
of racial melancholy to defensive and offensive strategies respectively, communal survival and consolidation. Perhaps Parks's and Kushner's plays are
designed to loosen the grip of this melancholy, forging interracial community
in resistance to its psychical and social effects.[3]

It is important to remember that Parks's and Kushner's plays—which were
published in 1996 and 2004, respectively—explore quite different moments
in modern social history of race and ideology. Parks's *Venus* depicts an early-
nineteenth-century world in which the distinctiveness of black bodies fueled
the rise of the discourse of scientific racism. The play dramatizes the ideological death of Saartjie Baartman. Baartman was lured from her home in Africa
and brought to Europe to reinforce biological notions of racial difference.
Baartman became the main attraction of Paris and London exhibitions in
the nineteenth century. Parks's early 1810s London is a meditation on a long

history of racial ideology that situates the black body as the West's locus of racial and sexual alterity. "Blackness" furnished the baseline against which normative social and sexual relations were forged and policed over time through the cultural practice of racism. At the same time, the discourses of racial and sexual difference reinforced one another's terms, reducing notions of racial difference to facts of the body. Accordingly, both black and normative bodies were left with little agency within the context of repetitive and ongoing social circumscription.[4] Therefore, Parks's *Venus* might be described as laying bare the social and ideological construction of whiteness and blackness as binary oppositions, rife with lost and disavowed social possibilities.

Kushner's *Caroline, or Change* depicts the pre–Civil Rights southern landscape occupied by those who suffer from what James Fisher has termed "the submerged oppression of middle-class American life," directly and indirectly (*Theater of Tony Kushner*, 198). The African Americans in Kushner's southern Louisiana, however, are positioned on the brink of racial progress. Indeed, Kushner's 1960s America in transition is one in which separate-but-equal segregation laws are fragile yet still in place. Moreover, unlike Venus and the host of characters who ensnare her in a sort of ideological death, the African American characters in *Caroline, or Change* are amid a large contingency of people dedicated to pronouncing their humanism by way of supporting nonviolent civil-rights demonstrations. The fact that this period of transition and severe racial strife was largely fueled by nonviolent direct action on the part of civil-rights demonstrators is not without significance. In this respect, Kushner's play sets a stage beyond the ambivalent power of ritual to forge and dismantle community amid differential power relations.

The force of both plays resides in the mindfulness they promote among theatergoers affectively linked by ideology and its attendant rituals. Indeed, this intersubjectivity is a condition in which the social and personal, historical and contemporary, latent and manifest overlap in ways that render moving through hidden affect and mourning disavowed social loss a great challenge. How did these playwrights convert theater into a form of cultural practice that engages and undermines the psychical legacy effects of the age of racial conservatism? If the complexities of intersubjectivity point to the impossibility of disaggregating and mourning historical and contemporary social loss, is the prospect of moving beyond racial melancholy and race doomed? How can we do so in community through theater? In what follows, I read Parks's *Venus* and Kushner's *Caroline, or Change* as forms of cultural practice that straddle the boundary between art and ritual to alter the theatergoer's engagement with the claims of our racial past through mourning and mindfulness.

Our attempts to build a more inclusive age of multiculturalism require more critical thinking about the disavowed psychical and material inscriptions of the age of racial conservatism. The current need to shift our attention from the promotion of "multicultural competencies" to "multicultural proficiency" suggests that moving beyond disavowed losses of self is ongoing, collective work that requires a unique blend of knowledge, awareness, and skills. Jonathan Flatley points out that "affective mapping"—that is, connecting with melancholic loss—must be promoted by aesthetic practice if we are to convert "a depressive melancholia into a way to be interested in the world" (*Affective Mappings*, 2). Changing our relationship with difference in the world requires the knowledge-based shift Flatley acknowledges and equally important awareness and skill-based components: seeing one's own social loss and acting on one's social possibilities within the broader context of affectively linked subject-formations. Parks's and Kushner's plays provide contexts for theatergoers to neutralize the psychic and social effects of racial melancholia within the interracial encounter.

Through an account of the unresolved racial grief that claims contemporary American theatergoers, my analysis of Suzan-Lori Parks's *Venus* and Tony Kushner's *Caroline, or Change* contemplates how cultural practice might be used to cut through and deactivate the unresolved grief that consolidates the racial divide in interracial community. This chapter builds on a short theoretical account of the sexual and cultural underpinnings of the discourse of racial difference to consider the unique role contemporary theater might play in exhuming and mourning the social loss it has consolidated. To that end, my analysis draws on the racial scene and unseen to situate the plays as art of profound cultural change. Parks's and Kushner's plays enact racial conflict to unearth disavowed social losses and assign them ideological origins. The plays uniquely allow spectators to explore what Kobena Mercer calls "those messy spaces in-between" black and white and acknowledge the culturally embedded web of gender, sexual, economic, and religious anxieties and prohibitions that discreetly underpin the discourse of racial difference and contemporary racial grievances (*Welcome to the Jungle*, 209). In doing so, Parks's and Kushner's plays summon and neutralize the disavowed social loss and hidden affect that structure our racial identifications to engender a coalition of racial grieving.[5]

Staging the Black Body, Racial Grieving, and Community

At the dawn of the twentieth century, often referred to as the Progressive Era, W. E. B. DuBois writes the "African American" subject-formation into social history. DuBois linked "self-conscious manhood" not only to the black sub-jects' African heritage but also to the denial of rights afforded white citizens (*Souls of Black Folk*, 5). Lacking the full rights and privilege of citizenship, the modern black subject's striving for a "truer self" in a segregationist society gives way to, according to DuBois, a peculiar psychical dissonance:

> It is a peculiar sensation, this double consciousness, this sense of always looking at oneself through the eyes of others, of measuring one's soul by the tape of a world that looks on in amused contempt and pity. One ever feels his two-ness,—an American, a Negro; two souls, two thoughts, two unreconciled strivings; two warring ideals in one dark body, whose dogged strength alone keeps it from being torn asunder. (45)

The inability to secure this synthesis, as both a "Negro" and "American," endures, even after anthropology exposed the status of race as a discursive formation during the early twentieth century and civil rights were granted to African Americans in the 1960s.

In *Becoming Black*, Michelle Wright reminds us that "double consciousness is not in fact the state of the DuBoisian subject but that the veil, produced by a materialist—rather than an idealist—'negation of the negation' is used in *Souls* to both critique the limits of the idealist dialectic and demonstrate that the Black operates both within and without the discourse of the white subject and Black Other" (69). If race is constructed and organized beyond the realm of discourse, it follows that social practice is partly responsible for the endurance of double consciousness. What is more, it follows that the national prohibition against miscegenation is responsible for the discourse of racial difference that gave birth to double consciousness in the first place. The cultural prohibition against sexual relations across the "color line" is not only a central thematic concern in Parks's *Venus* but the access point through which the play's theoretical agenda—that is, mourning the social losses that attend this cultural work—is forged.

In *Playing in the Dark*, Toni Morrison identifies an "Africanist presence" as the formative yet disavowed "ghost in the machine" of the American lit-erary canon (5). For Morrison, the paradox of *black presence yet exclusion* so prevalent in the American literary canon mirrors the racial politics that forged American nationhood. For Morrison, there is a ghost of the age of racial conservatism that haunts contemporary race relations that must be exorcised in order to move forward. "All of us, white and black, northern and southern" Grace Elizabeth Hale adds, should think of the south and the nation's "race problem" as a burden that is not of a "dark and distant place" but "as a burden that we still carry as a history that we have not agreed or acknowledged as a source of our subjectivities" (*Making Whiteness*, 295). How might theater help us untangle and better manage these affective remains? How does Parks's invitation to revisit the prevalent yet unlawful sexual relationships between antebellum white males and black females serve as a starting point for this disentanglement?

The exhibition of Baartman in the museums of Europe, according to Rosemarie Thompson, served as the cultural foundation of racial and sexual alterity upon which normative gender and sexual codes in the West were negotiated (*Extraordinary Bodies*, 70). This "ape-like" figure, according to Thompson, embodied the baseline of humanity against which gender and sexual ideals and terms of engagement were stabilized, and black bodies were policed in the name of advancing "civilized" culture, according to Thompson (71). The image of the free-ranging and unruly black female body pervaded the iconography of the Victorian era to at once tighten the regulation of the social and sexual behavior of white women and secure their privileged status as "sexually pure" within the nation's chivalric code. Michele Wallace points out that "Visual differentiation was the foundation of most thought about race and sexuality" during the age of racial conservatism, and this differentiation was mobilized by "the spectatorial imagination of the West, the gaze, the need to study and examine the other" ("The Hottentot Venus," 31). By publishing and thereby exaggerating the differences between black and white bodies, visual modernity served to feed the social and economic interests of Western nations. The West's particular interest in objectifying the black female body was grounded in both social and economic interests and the disavowal of denied kinship relations between antebellum blacks and whites. Thus, Parks's dramatization of the ideological death of Baartman exhumes a lie buried under Western cultural logic: the prevailing discourse of racial difference. The disgust Baartman's archetypal body engenders in the West is affect that covers shame and guilt that attends centuries of denied "mixed-blood" progeny born and reared in the service of the institution of slavery.

Parks's staging of Baartman's oversized posterior implicates theatergoers in the forces of social, economic, and national progress that occasioned her early death.[6] Spectators are arrested and bound by the sight of Baartman's oversized posterior. The implication is that we cannot put the history of racialization behind us because we carry this history in our racialized gaze as we move forward and plot futures. We might say that melancholic normative subjects are always in search of the other they associate with taboo social and sexual relations and disavow as historical underpinnings of their social identifications. The process of undoing the hold of racial melancholy's social constraints begins with Venus's archetypal black body. Parks directs the theatergoers' gaze toward Venus's body and their individual and collective social losses at once.

Through *Venus*, art rubs against melancholic life to collapse the boundary between theater performance and the theatergoer's performativity to promote critical race consciousness. David Krasner reminds us that "We 'rub elbows' in life, and in the theater we extend this idea of social interaction further. . . . As observer, I take the action of another as the material for standards of criteria of selfhood. In doing so, I place myself imaginatively in another situation" ("Empathy in Theater," 255–77). This overlap gives way to a chain of anticipation and pregnant pauses that implicate theatergoers in the play's conflict and its missing resolution. By opening up a theoretical space through which to resist the actor-audience binary, Krasner points to the ideological function of theater. Since audience members can be prompted to process theatrical events and circumstances in a manner that locates the self center-stage, it follows that the medium carries the capacity to resolve internal tensions and conflicts within by way of the "watching self" and interaction with "others." Like ritual, theater has the capacity to influence how theatergoers view and mold themselves, "capable of taking people through changes" (Cohen-Cruz, *Local Acts,* 101). Deborah R. Geis points out how several productions of *Venus* use the play's circus aspects—intrusive lights, view obstructing lattice of plain and patterned strings—which demand a closer look and cause audience members to question their own participation in the exploitation depicted on stage (*Suzan-Lori Parks,* 83). Such alterations, moreover, can be designed specifically by playwrights to change how the individual interacts with others. Thus, the theater experience stimulates the indeterminacy of subject-formations, compromising the integrity of their melancholic constitutions.[7] The notion of building community through collective mourning frees the work of these playwrights from the racial identity politics that often attend literary and cultural studies. As a result, *Venus* and *Caroline, or Change* function as artistic responses to the racial essentialism that ignores the critical role cultural production plays in forging a shared future for all members of a diverse republic.

Toward a Shared Future: Parks's and Kushner's Art of Ritual

The debate over the role the audience plays in determining the value and meaning of literature stems back to ancient Greece. For instance, in their 335 BC dialogue concerning the origins and effects of literature, relayed in *Poetics,* we learn that Plato and Aristotle advocate divergent points of view.

Literature, Aristotle reminds Plato, is not only far from value-free, but neither do its effects exist in a vacuum, isolated from the reader's response. For Plato, spectators stood as empty vessels through which meaning was transferred wholesale. Aristotle argued against Plato's theory of mimetic realism, locating the spectator's response as a vehicle for the transmission of the author's artistic worldview.

The disagreement between Plato and Aristotle about the function and afterlife of art has taken on an even more complicated permutation in recent years. In "Getting the Spirit," his introduction to *The Fire This Time*, Harry J. Elam Jr. complicates Aristotle's critique of Plato's conventional mimetic realism, recalling one of James Baldwin's declarations: "mirrors can lie."[8] Elam recalls the way Anna Deavere Smith takes the force of mimetic realism to task in her historical revisionist text, *Fires in the Mirror* (1997). Smith's play (first performed in 1992), Elam notes, "holds a mirror up to [representations of reality], but also reveals how cultural baggage, history, and religion all shape our ongoing negotiations of identity and therefore what we see in the mirror. Refraction can enable one to see more deeply perhaps, but also to misrecognize the subject" ("Getting the Spirit," xvi). "Truth" is thus generated and renegotiated by an ongoing theatrical and revision process. In this regard, the quest to get at the "truth" is futile. What we are given, then, in the theatrical display, is an opportunity to engage with the past on our own terms.

According to Jan Cohen-Cruz, "As society changes, so does the nature of radical politics and so must the role of socially conscious art" (*Local Acts*, 51). Indeed, Parks's and Kushner's plays do not advance the identity politics that informed their production. As Cohen-Cruz reminds us, "Much performance in the late 1960s and into the 1970s was shaped by identity politics, the organization of people around one core aspect of who they are in terms such as race and ethnicity" (49). Staging plays for a nation united under racial melancholy, Parks and Kushner provided contexts for theatergoers to recognize and renegotiate present and future lives of historical entrapment.

Much like the opening of Toni Morrison's *Beloved*, the audiences of Parks's *Venus* and Kushner's *Caroline, or Change* are snatched up and suspended by plays that demand and defy immediate decoding. Through the dramatization of black womanhood, Parks and Kushner place theatergoers on the boundary between their desire to know and the fear of greater understanding of the mutually constitutive relationship between the self and otherness. Theatergoers endure the unrelenting social and historical tides, rocking back and forth between knowing and impossible knowing. Theatergoers are invited to identify or disidentify with Venus and Caroline, the central characters of the plays. These identifications or disidentifications are empathic passages that seduce theatergoers into bed with the underside of history. There is no rest for theatergoers within the bowels of Parks's and Kushner's metaphorical ships of time travel into social history because they are placed between the sheets of the discourse of racial difference. Here, tidy articulations of the discourse of racial difference mesh into a sort of haze that cannot be moved through or understood by the theatergoer at once. Its primary purpose is to prompt the theatergoer to wrestle with a disremembered social history— sex and lies, renewal and reputation, philanthropy and economy, research and scientific racism, longing and fear—muffled by the crashing clamor of received knowledge and stereotypes.

Scholars who write about the formation and maintenance of a normative American nationhood during and after the Reconstruction Era rarely discuss its melancholic underpinnings and permutations. The frequency of racism and the inability to name and discuss the damage of racism are melancholic responses to social losses disavowed under the weight of visual modernity's representational authority. As Cheng reminds us, "it can be damaging to say how damaging racism has been" (*Melancholy of Race,* 14). Avoiding this potential damage ironically forges racial community and undermines interracial community. In the process, emotions are felt and suppressed as identities are constructed and filled with disavowed social losses. Parks and Kushner plot paths shot through the conscionable and hidden affect toward the myriad and disavowed social losses that undermine interracial community. Walking this path from opposition to partnership, Parks and Kushner suggest, will come at a price to all who define selfhood through the prism of biological notions of racial difference.

Seeing Ourselves in Parks's Freak Show

By dramatizing the objectification of Saartjie Baartman through the figure of Venus, Parks sparks a critical debate on the problematic nature of representing the pained black body in our contemporary multiculture.[9] I read the controversy over Parks's staging of the figure of Baartman as one of the legacy effects of our ongoing investment in biological notions of racial difference. Moreover, the persistence of racial essentialism in the more inclusive age of multiculturalism is the result of a cultural inability to extinguish racial grievances in the face of our clamor for racial progress in a white supremacist society. In this sense, racial identifications stand as proxies for unresolved grief exacerbated through rituals of racial policing and resistance. "Like melancholia," Cheng argues, "racism is hardly ever a clear rejection of the other. While racism is mostly thought of as a kind of violent rejection of the other, racist institutions in fact often do not want to fully expel the racial other" (12). Parks's play also links the ritualized rejection of the other to the discourse of family and normality that underpins nation formation and cohesion. Through this unveiling, the play pushes theatergoers beyond the hidden affective states and social losses that wash ashore when identifications rooted discreetly in nationalist agendas are exposed as such.[10]

Parks's reobjectification of Baartman links authority's ambivalent relationship with difference to a context-specific and volatile marketplace of desire. In doing so, Parks renders the contingency and indeterminacy of social meaning palpable and, as a result, negotiable for theatergoers.[11] Theatergoers are also given the chance to understand the mutually constitutive nature of their racial identities. When all of this becomes conscionable on the level of human experience, a theater-based grieving ensues. Grieving the social losses that attend one's racial identity makes it possible for theatergoers to exercise discernment in intercultural contexts that might otherwise end in melancholic scripting, racial subjugation, and social collapse.

Be My Tragic Valentine

Ultimately, Venus's insatiable desire for love, power, and money stand as a melancholic effect, a means of repudiating the social loss and despair it breeds. Venus puts her heart on the line to secure the love of the Baron Docteur. Standing as the play's locus of white heteropatriarchal authority, purity, and promise, the Baron Docteur cannot deliver the love, power, and money promised to Venus. Venus's assimilation crisis hinges on the Baron Docteur's desire-inducing symbolization of all she cannot embody yet conditions. Neither the Baron Doctor nor Venus can be saved from the racial stereotyping from which "there is no escape" (*Venus*, 42). Depicting Venus's desire to eat chocolate she cannot stomach, Parks allegorizes Venus's internalization of racial ideology propelled by the transatlantic trading economy of black bodies and sugar. Geis remarks, "Feeding Venus chocolates not only keeps her subservient, but also instills the sense that if she is to have any agency, it must involve, ironically, maintaining the image of herself as a fetishized object" (*Suzan-Lori Parks*, 94). The Baron Docteur tries yet fails to get Venus to recognize that she is "eating her heart out": "Upset stomach? I'll fix you something, you eat too many chocoluts you know. I give em to you by the truckloads but you don't have to eat them all. Practice some restraint. Drink this" (*Venus*, 127). The irony of the Baron Docteur's observation issues a reminder for all theatergoers: The psychological appeal and threat of whiteness for nonwhites is its intangibility. Nevertheless, Venus feeds on her futile quest for power and success: "We'll set tongues wagon for the rest of the century. The Docteur will introduce me to Napoléan himself. Oh, yes your Royal Highness the Negro question does keep me awake at night oh yes it does. Servant girl! Do this and that! When I'm mistress I'll be a tough cookie. I'll rule the house with an iron fist and have the most fabulous parties. Hhhh . . . I need a new wig" (135). Melancholics, Freud tells us, display a "trait of insistent communicativeness which finds satisfaction in self-exposure" ("Mourning and Melancholia," 585). Venus's pained body clearly needs soothing; her self-indulgence and arrogance, however, are melancholic responses to a low self-image she suppresses with great difficulty. Her internalized inferiority and its attendant modes of compensation are social and historically scripted symptoms of racial melancholy.

While this melancholic response is beyond Venus's conscious recognition, Parks allows theatergoers to step into her melancholic cast of mind. According to Geis, "When the spectators of the Oberlin production were thrown chocolates during the intermission, their consumption of Venus as the object of the gaze became more than just visual; their eagerness to 'digest' was mocked even as they were being soothed or placated with food" (*Suzan-Lori Parks*, 94). Theatergoers may be inclined to identify or disidentify with Venus's lack of agency amid dominant authority; nevertheless, Parks provides a context for them to explore and reflect on their own lack of agency within the New World of commodified black bodies. Eating the same "chocoluts," theatergoers are positioned to connect with their own plights of impossible mourning generated within the context of the age of racial conservatism. The unsettling effect of being accomplices to the mockery they are subject to stages an empathic passage for theatergoers to escape the performative effects of racial melancholia in their lives beyond the theater house. Moving theatergoers past racial shame to self-awareness within the broader historical context of racial scripting emerges as the critical force of the play's work of collective grieving.

Grieving in the Name of Love

The thrust of the collective racial grieving that *Venus* promotes resides in its depiction of economically determined racial scripting. Like the Baron Docteur, the Negro Resurrectionist is trapped in a system where his survival is linked to the exploitation of a more visible Other. Paralyzed by the looming threat of the "thugh slammer," the Negro Resurrectionist's moral compass sinks to a low place: all respect for the dead's need to rest in peace is lost (159). The Negro Resurrectionist thus is the accomplice to the exploitation of Venus in death and stands as the play's locus of humanism that evades the workings of power. Parks makes a moral appeal to theatergoers through the Negro Resurrectionist's failed moral conscience. The theatergoer is left to look for the absent scraps of moral fiber left behind the scene. The Negro Resurrectionist's indifference to the proper burial of the remains of Venus is born out of the racial essentialism that also motivates and mobilizes racial identification itself. The Imperial West has historically coped with the contradiction of racism in a nation premised on equality through scientific racism, the most ubiquitous yet aggressive ritual of cultural melancholy. Clearly, the Negro Resurrectionist is more attuned to the material advantages of scientific racism than to its moral implications: "I used to dig up people/ dead ones. You know,/ after theyd been buried. Doctors pay a lot for corpses/ but "Resurrection" is illegal/ and I was always this close to getting arrested. / This Jail-Watchman's job much more carefree" (158). Indeed, theatergoers are hard pressed to deny living under the shadow of scientific racism's influence on U.S. public policy, the criminal justice system, and consumer capitalism. If the life and body of Baartman are to be properly memorialized, Parks suggests that those who *have* and *have not* benefited from her marginalization and exploitation must acknowledge the mutual indispensability and economic determinants of their fates.

By closing the text without reconciliation, Parks leaves the unfinished work of grieving the lost social possibilities that attend the history of scientific racism squarely in the laps of theatergoers. At the beginning of the play, before the "Hottentot" is pronounced ideologically dead, theatergoers are directed to survey her anatomical differences, as she turns counter clockwise. Here is the take home message: normative and minority theatergoers are more invested in a view of the "Hottentot's" difference than they can acknowledge. The idea of beginning at the end is to strongly suggest that we are entrapped in our historical past. Parks ends the play without laying Baartman to rest because there is no imaginative plot big enough to furnish a proper burial for the subjective remains of the legacy of the mutually reinforcing discourses of racial and sexual difference. This re-objectification of Baartman is not an artistic risk but a means to a more progressive end. *Venus*, the play, is a model of cultural production that does not encourage moving beyond the past but advocates engaging its unbearable legacy of unmourned social loss directly so that we might navigate its melancholic symptoms with discernment.

The play concludes with Venus standing before the audience pleading for true love's kiss: "*Kiss me Kiss me Kiss me Kiss*" (162). I read this request to lock lips as a call to move forward in full acknowledgement of our mutually constitutive and unresolved racial grief. While the social and economic conditions that gave rise to Baartman's status as the icon of Western scientific racism remain with us, the denial, indifference, and righteousness they secured along the way are untapped communal resources for building a shared future. Parks's play provides convincing evidence that the arts are critically important arenas where we might mine the psychic effects of an unruly racial past for critical self-awareness and communal engagement.

Household Rules, Quiet Victories, and Little Tragedies: *Caroline, or Change*

The world of Parks's *Venus* is one of burgeoning racialization. In contrast, Tony Kushner's semiautobiographical musical, *Caroline, or Change*, depicts a 1960s world of legalized racial segregation. On the eve of the assassination of President John F. Kennedy and the Civil Rights Act of 1964, racial tensions are high in Kushner's fictional world, and the veneer of civility within and between social categories gives way to unlikely bonds and social tragedies. A Jewish American household living in Lake Charles, Louisiana, the Gellmans' symbolic incorporation into the American fold of cross-class white racial sameness was accompanied by a luxury tax. In this fragile social climate, a simple household rule designed to socially and financially discipline the youngest member of the Gellman family becomes a catalyst for a loss of the profoundest sort.

In the play's title character, Caroline Thibodeaux, theatergoers are presented the embodiment of black disenfranchisement in the material, symbolic, and disavowed service of securing "normality" for a growing number of white ethnics. Theatergoers quickly learn the severe degree to which this unacknowledged social work has undermined the spirit of the play's marginalized black domestic worker. As James Fisher observes, "To survive her grief, Caroline closes off her emotions; she goes on but in a detached state in which she can function in the muteness of domestic slavery, a slavery not ended for black women even a hundred years after the Civil War" (*Understanding Tony Kushner*, 91). Existing in a world that leaves little room for the enfranchisement of the black community, Caroline swallows her bitterness in exchange for "loose change" (*Caroline, or Change*, 45). "Loose change" is the play's metaphor for monetary compensation that does not support the standard of living and well-being reserved for whites. One might expect to find the white beneficiaries of American capital and state to be swaddled in bliss; but Kushner tethers a little tragedy to the Gellman's reach for white ethnic anonymity in domesticity.

There's a social history that prefigures Caroline and Noah's acquaintanceship that must be handled with care for the sake of a shared future. As Kushner explains, "This play comes from sorrow, from anger and grief, and also from hope learned from history, from recent history, which has shown us that change, progress, is difficult, uneven, uncertain, but also absolutely possible" (**xv**). By hinging the well-being of Caroline's family on Noah's fiscal irresponsibility, Kushner holds a cracked mirror to the surface of any claims to civility that do not wed social and economic justice. Indeed, Caroline's social context is indifferent to her growth and development. Through the depiction of overlapping and competing trajectories of choice, personal security, and loss, Kushner enlists theatergoers as witnessing participants in the play's critique of liberal nationalism. The play insists on a critique of a nation that curbs its religious intolerance in the name of promoting and securing a normative social body through exclusion.

Without Sanctuary

The despair of disenfranchised blueswomen like Caroline cannot be fully itemized, contained, or contextualized. At once a psychical and social interdiction, Caroline's unresolved grief is grounded in authority's uneven and contradictory response to the nation's social aspirations.[12] As Daryl Michael Scott notes, social liberals and conservatives of the Progressive Era nationhood believed emancipation exacerbated the mental health issues African Americans faced under racial slavery (*Contempt and Pity*, 13). Just beneath the surface of Rose's civility, theatergoers find contempt for the disenfranchised:

> I'm just trying to help you,
> you know, with the money.
> It was only a game.
> (*Aside:*)
> So sue me already,
> Miss Crabby Appleton!
> I don't know what's eating you!
> Some people, honestly!
> There's oppression and misery,
> And then there are people
> who're just plain nasty.
> (*To Caroline:*)
> Just trying to be friendly.
> Just trying to be a friend. (*Caroline, or Change*, 78)

Rose's tutorial in fiscal responsibility for her man-in-training is designed subconsciously to wedge herself between Noah and Caroline. As a result, her contempt for Caroline is a cover for her self-contempt.

The rift Rose wedges between Noah and Caroline opens space for theater-goers to see that quite a bit "happens under ground in Louisiana" (11). In the section "Lot's Wife," theatergoers learn that Caroline is conditioned to carry Rose's displaced burden of proof: "My madness rise up in a fury so wild and I let myself go. / Spoke my hate to a child" (116). Caroline's mind-numbing attachment to labor below the water table allegorizes the mix of self-depre-ciation, sorrow, and unrequited desire she fights to sublimate. Kushner relies on anthropomorphic figures to personify and distill the layers of Caroline's hidden affect for theatergoers. Every day, Caroline visits the basement of the Gellman household, where she fights against these emotions to avoid em-bracing the nagging layers of social loss personified by the washing machine, radio, and dryer.

Caroline and Noah's unresolved racial grievances are historically and so-cially constructed. In the Gellman household, bonds between stepmother and child, father and son, and husband and wife are tenuous. The religious an-tagonism that motivated the assassination of President John F. Kennedy only exacerbated racial anxiety among Jewish American families of the era of pro-tean change. The Stopnick-Gellman family curbs this anxiety through rituals of fiscal conservatism. Just after Mr. Stopnick hands Noah the controversial twenty-dollar bill, he issues a warning: Noah! /Never forget!" (*Caroline, or Change*, 95). In this six-syllable utterance melancholy is transferred across a generation; indeed, Mr. Stopnick buries the collective social loss incurred through the long history of European anti-Semitism in Noah's psychic life. Despite being a foreigner to this social history, Noah is indoctrinated eas-ily into his family's legacy of fiscal conservatism. It is this ghost of Jewish-American-redemption-and-assimilation-on-economic-terms that haunts Noah's speech act of racialization against Caroline: "I HATE YOU! I HATE YOU! I HATE YOU! There's a bomb! President Johnson has built a bomb/ special made to kill all Negroes! / I hate you, hate you, kill all Negroes! Really! For true! / I hope he drops his bomb on you!" (104). Noah's identification with his grandfather's economic shrewdness secures a familial bond that propagates the racial antagonism upon which it is predicated. The racial rift between Noah and Caroline is swaddled in the Jewish American struggle for cultural redemption and assimilation. Noah and Caroline's broken bond is a social tragedy. Noah, like Caroline, is without sanctuary.

Noah's freshly minted fiscal conservatism is accompanied by a lesson in social liberalism: "The Negro maid, she's making bupkes, how does that look, leaving change in his pockets?" (26). Pitting Caroline's economic gain against the development of Noah's moral consciousness loads the dice against their camaraderie. This ad hoc approach to increasing Caroline's salary undermines her self-respect. Moreover, the "Aftermath" section suggests that a prison house of liberal white racial guilt is just around the corner from the house of white racial self-interest. "I did it. I killed her. I did it she died," Noah explains (108). Acting as an agent of familial cohesion and white-ethnic assimilation, Noah's self-concept is thus eternally racialized. Noah's role of racial oppressor is linked to his concept of self. Noah will never be the same again; his race and self-concept are one. Noah hides the guilt that attends his racial self in the arrogance that undergirds white racial authority. All of this constructedness gives way to circumstances that far outstrip Noah's life and consequences that "have not yet arrived" (xv).

In *Caroline, or Change*, racialized selfhood is grounded in social, economic, and historical processes. Through the figure of Noah, theatergoers see this transgenerational transmission live. Mr. Stopnick reminds Rose to recognize the obvious and necessary: "No, you're the boss. . . . It's hard, but not mean. You got in between. Maybe Rosie, now you can be his mother" (109–11). Mr. Stopnick positions Caroline's loss as Rose's gain. Thandeka might describe Rose's "gain" as "an attack against the child by members of its own white community because the child is not yet white" (18). Rose leaves Noah bereft of the humility and self-consciousness he will need in order to engage, critique, and revise his chosen mode of civic engagement. Indeed, "Household rules and small decrees unsuspectingly bring us these secret little tragedies" (123).

This absence of reflective democratic practice is one of the legacy effects of the Cartesian ontology that survived into the Civil Right era. The abstract individualism spawned by the Enlightenment—grounded in a lack of concern with one's connection with the living cosmos—worked through visual modernity to render "race" a proxy for the self. This disconnect and alienation are not only a part of being in the modern world but the breeding ground for the racial pride and arrogance that circumvents the personal awareness and knowledge of social history necessary for resuscitating ideological casualties.[13]

Even though Caroline and Noah are sure to share cigarettes in the future, they will do so under a false cover of civility. Kushner suspends Noah and Caroline in a pool of unresolved racial grief. This impasse is not only the lot of both Noah and Caroline, but any and all racialized subject-formations galvanized by nationalist prohibitions, anxieties, and stigmas.[14]

Noah and Caroline cannot forge a bond against a well-wrought racial caste system that prefigures and situates their places in the world. Like the impossible marriage between Venus and the Baron Docteur, Rose and Noah's intimacy ends before it begins. While this fractured bond crumbles at the first sign of conflict, theatergoers see how Caroline absorbs the economic shock of the fallout. In the section "Lot's Wife," Caroline is reduced to a shell of an existence, a life of service in a melancholic haze.

A Clearing Beyond the Haze

I would like to end this chapter with a brief discussion of the twilight space with which Kushner punctuates *Caroline, or Change*. In the section "Emmie's Dream," somewhere between the darkness of the past and the promise of future, theatergoers learn that pluralism depends on our ability to work through the psychical claims of history. It is the figure of Emmie who models "mind over matter" and paves a path beyond history's claims on racial subjectivity. Emmie knows that the promise of democratic civic engagement across the color line can be extinguished by the historical amnesia that haunts the "American way." At the same time, Emmie warns against confusing the embrace of social memory with being haunted by one's history:

> "I'm the daughter of a maid,
> in her uniform, crisp and clean!
> Nothing can ever make me afraid!
> You can't hold on, you Nightmare Men,
> your time is past now on your way
> get gone and never come again!
> For change come fast and change come slow but
> everything changes!
> And you got to go!"
> Shout shout Devil on
> Out!! (*Caroline, or Change*, 126)

The image of Emmie in a nightgown on the sparkling green lawn foreshadows a future that exists harmoniously with the past. Caroline's inability to strike this crucial balance and her resulting brokenness serves Emmie and theatergoers pedagogically. More specifically, unlike her mother, who dressed daily in crisp white, Emmie is not starched by the past and manages to use it to bend into future possibilities. Ultimately, the figure of Emmie not only challenges the Freudian divide between mourning and melancholia but also suggests that their ongoing engagement provides the grounds upon which racialized subjects might exploit the indeterminacy of social meaning for the common good.

In *The Psychic Life of Power*, Judith Butler notes that there is no final separation of mourning from melancholia. Indeed, there is no reprieve from the psychic ambivalence that attends this impossible binary. Butler makes the point, "Ambivalence, which is first identified as a possible response to loss in 'Mourning and Melancholia,' becomes, toward the end of the essay, the struggle that loss occasions between the desire to live and the desire to die. As such, both ambivalence and the struggle of life and death, to borrow Hegelian parlance, are occasioned by loss, indeed, instigated by loss. If ambivalence distinguishes melancholia from mourning, and if mourning entails ambivalence as part of the process of 'working through,' then there is no work of mourning that does not engage melancholia" (193). Butler locates the subject as a being just as indeterminate as social meaning. Subject formation through language is an ongoing process that keeps the ego alive and in a perpetual state of reconstitution.

Emmie charts a path beyond the haze of melancholy through mourning. "Listen girlie, we have learned: nonviolence will get you burned," Mr. Stopnick explains to Emmie (*Caroline, or Change*, 90). He goes on to elaborate: "Why's it so impossible to know, white or Jew or Negro, if the bosses boot's in your face—what do you do? Shed a tear? Keep lying there? A face knows it's no footrest regardless of religion or race!" (91). Traumatized by the lived and remembered experience of death and anti-Semitism, Mr. Stopnick urges Emmie to see the futility of nonviolent approaches to cultural reclamation. Yet, as Emmie points out and theatergoers are primed to recognize, he acts in a vacuum isolated from civic responsibility and does not understand the things "Dr. King has planned." Emmie insists that Mr. Stopnick's cast of mind cripples his ability to offer Southern African Americans a strategic plan: "I'd like to know how/ some guy just off a plane/ marching in to explain,/ guess you see it all plain from the air?/ It's our/ affair./ Now our resistance starts to make a difference/here come your assistance" (91). For Emmie and theatergoers, Mr. Stopnick's eye-for-an-eye approach draws on the social history of race in a divisive way that reconstitutes melancholy as opposed to using it discerningly in the service of community building.

Emmie points to the underside of Mr. Stopnick's need to quantify resistance. In doing so, Emmie points to a condition that the lived threat of post-Emancipation racial subjugation works overtime to consolidate for members of social bodies who must tiptoe through life. Indeed, there is a genealogy of affect and social loss that travels through Caroline discreetly across a generation:

> Salting the earth so nothing grow
> Too close; but still her strong blood flow . . .
> Under ground through hidden veins,
> down from storm clouds when it rains,
> down the plains, down the high plateau,
> down to the Gulf of Mexico.
> Down to Larry and Emmie and Jackie and Joe.
> The children of Caroline Thibodeaux. (127)

Caroline's hidden veins are discreet, transgenerational passages; Emmie, Jackie, and Joe are on the receiving end of a mudslide of hidden affect. Nevertheless, theatergoers are placed in a frame of self-discovery and leave knowing that somehow it is possible to redirect the trajectory of their own melancholic subject-formations, "For change come fast and change come slow but/ everything changes!" (126).

I would like to resist any reading suggesting that Kushner leaves theatergoers unequipped to exploit racial melancholy for the common good.[15] Instead, I would insist on reading Emmie's recognition of the need to move through the racial melancholy she shares with her mother as proffering an empathic community primed to work through the subjective impact of the age of racial conservatism on our twenty-first-century multiculture. Through the figure of Emmie, Kushner's art of ritual creates a space for multiple responses toward the resolution of a shared condition. The ideological and subjective legacy of the age of racial conservatism has generated the egocentric inability to see difference as historically coded, and, moreover generative and value-added. Therefore, we must develop forms of cultural practice designed to promote communal agency in the full awareness of our social and historical contingency.

At a recent showing of *Caroline, or Change* I attended in Minneapolis, members of the interracial audience were moved to tears by the production. A white woman sitting beside me, sensing the social change in our midst, shook nervously as she took my hand and shared a revelation: "We are one, my foreign friend, we are one." The passion in her voice and eyes attested to how invested she was in dismantling the colonial scenario that compelled us to refrain from greeting one another upon taking our seats at the beginning of the play. At that moment, we looked at what Diana Taylor calls "the embodied apparition of colonial practices" in the face and terrorized it (*The Archive and the Repertoire*, 74).

Attempting to uncover a paradigm for understanding how we might circumvent Cartesian egotism in "Empathy and Theater," David Krasner recalls Maurice Merleau-Ponty's amendment of Husserl's "Cartesian solipsism" (I exist in my own inescapable world) position:

> Merleau-Ponty amends Husserl's position by emphasizing the transference of "corporeal" (embodied) existence in which my psyche and my awareness are "not a series of 'states of consciousness' that are rigorously closed in on themselves and inaccessible to anyone but me." Rather, my consciousness "is turned primarily toward the world, turned toward things; it is above all a relation to the world." (270)

This insight renders the content of the melancholic ego subject to perpetual evolution. This insight also denaturalizes the subject-formation, neutralizing false notions of singularity and stasis that strain our ability to build productive coalitions in the world as interdependent cohabitants.

Theater is a mechanism for the facilitation of embodied cultural practice, an interlocutor that connects the racialized theatergoer to the social and historical conditions he or she disavows as formative experiences of their own and unimagined communal possibilities. *Caroline, or Change* and *Venus* allow theatergoers to imagine one another at different and mutually determining locations within the field of cultural melancholy where they might reimagine a more aware and discerning community. Together, *Caroline, or Change* and *Venus* invite theatergoers to turn away from body politics and begin the hard work of imagining and co-creating a more pluralistic future that works through the hidden affect and social loss that attends subjection in language. Parks and Kushner suggest this is predicated on our willingness to engage in cultural practice that allows us to grieve and redeem social losses in the communal context that straddles the fence between art and ritual.

CODA

On Conformity to the Category of Time (Race)

"Our lives are not our own. We are bound to others, past
and present, and by each crime and every kindness, we
birth our future."
—David Mitchell, *Cloud Atlas*

At the end of the 2012 film *Cloud Atlas*, an elderly "biracial" couple, played
by Halle Berry and Tom Hanks, stand united in love far beyond what Frantz
Fanon calls "conformity to the categories of time" (4).[1] The epic science fiction
drama, produced and directed by Lana Wachowski, Tom Tykwer, and Andy
Wachowski, spans six eras charting multiple and interdependent trajectories
of crime against humanity and kindness that link past, present, and future.
In the first era, "The Pacific Journal of Adam Ewing" (1894), Hanks plays
Dr. Henry Goose, a sinister doctor who prepares to steal the valuables of
his patient, Adam Ewing, by disguising poison in what he claims to be a
cure for a parasitic worm. Just before the fatal dose is administered, Ewing
is saved by Autua, a stowaway slave. In gratitude, Ewing and his wife relin-
quish property rights to the plantation they are slated to inherit and join
the abolitionist movement. In the final era, "Sloosha's Crossin' an' Ev'rythin'
After" (2321), the spirit Hanks plays is reincarnated in the figure of Zachry.
Zachry lives in a primitive society called "The Valley," a postapocalyptic
colony of Earth. Zachry is presented with a choice: Before he can unite with
Meronym (played by Berry) in love, he must release his thoughts and actions
from the bondage of a demonic spirit of racism, greed, and fear called "Old
Georgie." What is instructive in this film is its insistence that the effects of
crimes against humanity span generations and social space yet can be extinguished and overcome in community. The climactic moment of the film's
dramatic plot structure is propelled by an ebb and flow in character of the

spirit Hanks plays in four incarnations. The spirit Hanks plays finds love, civic engagement, and community only after it learns to engage beyond the puppeteering of disavowed social loss and hidden affect that works through ritual to confiscate the present and future.

I began this project in hopes of exploring the tenacity and limits of the tyranny of what I have called "cultural melancholy" after watching the opening scene of Rhoda Grauer's *Dancing: New Worlds, New Forms*. Grauer's documentary provides a vivid and detailed account of an Afro-Brazilian Condomblé ritual. Here, a circle of bodies, bowed and lurched, tarry to raise the dead. This scene brought my mind's eye back to the Baptist church I visited as a young boy with my grandparents in the Mississippi Delta. The Afro-Brazilians' moment of contact between the living and dead strangely reflects what my grandparents referred to as "the moment of contact between the Holy Spirit and the living." The format of this Baptist ritual—fervent and extemporaneous movements that gradually grew out of calm, extended prayer sessions—mirrors that of the Afro-Brazilians' Condomblé ceremony. It was, therefore, through cross-cultural analysis, a curiosity about the intangible traces of the past within everyday life, and sheer intuition that I began the quest that took me to several archives, and which resulted in a dissertation at the University of Minnesota, two research grants, and currently a book on the dynamic.

More than 130 years have passed since the ratification of the Thirteenth Amendment to the U.S. Constitution declared slavery illegal in the United States. What I have attempted to demonstrate is that America still suffers from the immaterial dimensions of the legacy of slavery and ongoing racial subjugation it claims with great difficulty. The chapters of this book work in concert to elucidate the affective claims of the history of slavery and ongoing racial subjugation through a theory of cultural melancholy. In writing this book through a close reading of American and African American literatures and cultures, I hoped that the final product would at once reveal a culturally and historically specific paradigm that explains how unresolved racial grievances are transmitted transgenerationally by way of ritual practice and uncover a paradigm for understanding racialized subject formation that is simultaneously individualistic and interpersonal.

Eschewing outdated disciplinary boundaries and insisting on the possibility of productive collaborations between American and African American literatures and cultures and psychoanalytic theory, this book draws on theories of melancholia to ground the inability to disaggregate the psychic past and present in nationalist agendas and the rituals that work through Lacan's Symbolic to support and combat them. Reminding us that racial categories are far from static and primeval, Hortense Spiller's "'All the Things You Could Be by Now, If Sigmund Freud's Wife Was Your Mother'" positions psycho-analysis as a useful tool for understanding the "interior intersubjectivity" (149) of racialized subjects within the context of exterior social forms and conditions. I've drawn on psychoanalysis to reflect on how we might make use of the constructedness of racial categories that the critical framework has been accused of reifying. Reconceptualizing the agency of collaborative synergies across disciplinary silos is a project this book aims to promote.

Taking into account everything from James Baldwin's insistence that "our passion for categorization" has "boomeranged us into chaos" ("Everybody's Protest Novel," 1702), to Toni Morrison's assertion that the historical exclusion of "pariahs" of U.S. society is the economic and cultural preconditions of the unity and cohesiveness of the nation's normative social body, it is no wonder why the nation's contemporary relationship with racial categories has taken on an ambivalence of clinical proportions. Of interest in Baldwin's claim is the idea that our ongoing psychic and material investments in racial categories is more destructive than productive. The ritually maintained and propagated melancholy this project uncovers through a close reading of American and African American literatures and cultures has left us in a racial lurch somewhere between biologism and social construction. What I have attempted to articulate in *Cultural Melancholy* is that we are a nation of racialized subjects bound by the social and affective voids of our own histori-cal creation. Indeed, without picking up the pieces of our social and psychic fragmentation, we run the risk of forgoing our own progressive impulse to grow in the community. Fundamentally, this book works against our sanc-tioned ignorance and contempt for the "other." This surface affect is nothing more than misdirected and misrecognized grievances toward the social and economic demands of a nation that has historically struggled to cope with the conundrum of class and racial inequality amid a national narrative of liberty and justice for all. I have written this book in hopes of highlighting the unresolved racial grievances of the past and present that work through the coimplication of social, political, and psychical structures to determine how we see ourselves in relation to "others." Conservative and neoliberal media outlets seem critically aware of the nation's deficit on this front, play-ing the American public like puppets on a string against the backdrop of its unresolved racial grievances.

Let's consider, for instance, two recent scandals played out in and by the media. The public outrage that gave way to canceled business contracts and revoked merchandising and endorsement deals that immediately followed Paula Dean's admission, while under oath, of using the word "Nigger" in the past points directly to the deep-seated racial pain and guilt that rumbles just beneath the surface of our twenty-first-century multiculture. Dean's technical lynching, to borrow the famous words of Clarence Thomas, was a ritualized fortification of a national investment in avoiding honest talk about the social construct of race and reifying the stock logic and assumptions about black people the word connotes. In the end, after the firestorm of Facebook and Twitter posts, the discourse of racial difference remained stable against what the court of public opinion deemed an offense against the humanity of black people.

In our current climate of racial anxiety, as Michelle Alexander reminds us in her recently published book *The New Jim Crow*, advocates of "the control of African Americans through racial caste systems, such as slavery and Jim Crow" have "birthed yet another racial caste system in the United States: mass incarceration" of black men (16). In this racial climate, black men who merely breech social contract are deemed pariahs to be monitored and policed. Recently, Kevin Clash, the voice of Elmo, resigned from the Sesame Street Workshop amid a second allegation that accused the famed puppeteer of having sex with a minor. A resulting flood of YouTube video, Facebook messages, and Twitter tweets on the ordeal tell us more about humanity's crime than any wrongdoing of Clash himself. One YouTuber felt "tricked" after discovering that his beloved Elmo was "controlled" by a "fat black guy." The Web is rife with racist speech designed to at once color and arrest the trauma of the social instability Clash's tenure as Elmo presents. One can't help but wonder whether the power that underpins what is alleged to be a "pipeline of victims" (represented by the same attorney) leveling cases for cash against Clash is wielded from the same court of public opinion that draws on the discourse of racial difference to invalidate Obama's presidency and justify the violent killing of thirteen-year-old Trayvon Martin in 2012 and eighteen-year-old Michael Brown in 2014 by police officers.

It was not Clash's guilt of the charges of unlawful sexual conduct but the innuendo thereof that urged him to step down from his post as one of the key executive producers for the Sesame Street Workshop. In recent years, Elmo and Clash himself were increasingly growing into stand-ins for the Sesame Street brand itself. Clash's appearances on *The View* and *The Oprah Winfrey Show* followed a string of Emmy nominations and awards that span more than a decade. The recent documentary, *Being Elmo*, cataloging Clash's journey up from puppeteering in his mother's backyard to Sesame Street, catapulted the creative artist into a global star after winning the Sundance Film Festival's Special Jury Prize for U.S. Documentary. Before his fall from grace, Clash lived a relatively private life on the Upper West Side of Manhattan as an openly gay man. The recent unearthing of his apparent attraction to younger-looking adult men remixed the profitability of an age-old cocktail of racial and sexual paranoia that permeated the Reconstruction era. Indeed, the case of Clash against the court of normative opinion reminds us that we will never be free from the bondage of our racial past until representational authority makes room for our dearest memories of childhood and innocence to be connected to blackness.

The culture of antagonism that emerged from the Dean and Clash controversies point to deep-seated attachments to historical narratives of racial difference that call for reflective pause and collective racial grieving. There is a massive chasm between everyday rituals of racialization and our social possibilities that must be filled. The quest to move beyond the nation's seemingly impervious melancholic haze requires us to exhume and resuscitate the lost selves lodged in our collective fear of letting go of the fixed realities and projections of the racialized mindset. I only hope this book stimulates the critical race consciousness required to disrupt our national conformity to outdated and unproductive categories of time.

NOTES

Introduction

1. Lisa Lowe, in *Immigrant Acts*, also links "loss that cannot be named and mourned" to "cultural dimensions of contemporary consequence" (139).

2. In recent years, works that interrogate the intersections between race and psychoanalysis have become prominent topics of discussion. In its concern with the psychical and social remains of the dead, my study locates itself within the existing psychoanalytic tradition that underscores the role of disavowed social loss and hidden affect in circumventing and obstructing the process of working through the legacy of racial slavery and imperialism. For example, both Anne Anlin Cheng's *The Melancholy of Race* and Paul Gilroy's *Postcolonial Melancholia* show us not only the importance of exploring the presence of the ghost of our imperial and colonial past in everyday political, social, and psychical life, but stress the central role of such insight and reflection in broadening the quality of civic life in our current multiculture "at ease with grievances but not with grief." Drawing on Judith Butler's theory of gender performativity (see *Gender Trouble*), which asserts that the strength of the subject lies in its fragility and inventiveness, this study explores how the ongoing performance of sameness and difference through which the racial melancholic consolidates itself also propagates hidden affect across time and social space.

3. In *The Melancholy of Race*, Anne Anlin Cheng notes that Freud's "Mourning and Melancholia" uncharacteristically accounts for losses beyond those of erotic frustration, losses ranging "from the actual death of the loved person or ideal to imagined disappointments" (199).

4. bell hooks, "Postmodern Blackness," in *Yearning: Race, Gender, and Cultural Politics*, 29. Turning our attention to the role cultural practice plays in African America's impossible mourning is especially important. Questions of ritual practice must be considered in relation to the waning of affect-based critiques of race, which have

shored up in the name of African American cultural reclamation. According to Phillip Novak in "'Circles and Circles of Sorrow': In the Wake of Morrison's Sula," "Because African American culture is still at risk, getting done with grieving might well constitute a surrender to the forces that produced the losses in the first place" (193). I will return to this issue of impossible mourning at the intersection of individual and collective subject formation and ritual practice to explore questions Novak generates yet does not answer: Is this melancholy static, confined to the subject-formation, or, rather, does it move across time and social space? What are the gendered and sexual effects of this impossible mourning as it impacts subject formation? What roles does ritual practice play in this dynamic? What implication does all of this carry for understanding the process of subject formation as both individualistic and interpersonal? Chapter 2, "Reconstituted Melancholy," puts psychoanalytic theorizations of Sigmund Freud's concept of melancholia and Jacques Derrida's poststructuralist reading of Karl Marx's work on specters in conversation with Wilson's *Piano Lesson* to take a closer look at the underpinnings of the cultural melancholy that claims post-Emancipation African American subject-formations and cultures.

5. See Anne McClintock's *Imperial Leather* for a discussion that links the "disciplinary quarantine of psychoanalysis from history" to "imperial modernity" (8).

6. For two of the most articulate examples, see Barbara Christian, "The Race for Theory" (280–89), and Joyce A. Joyce, "'Who the Cap Fit': Unconsciousness and Unconscionableness in the Criticism of Houston A. Baker Jr. and Henry Louis Gates Jr." (319–30).

7. In "Music and Melancholy," Gary Rosenshield draws on Anton Chekhov's "Rothschild's Fiddle" to problematize Baldwin's attribution of Sonny's blues to both personal and social conditions. What strikes me about Rosenshield's analysis is his equation of Baldwin and the unnamed narrator in "Sonny's Blues," noting how the writer "supersede[s] his narrator" and tells the "meaning of the blues poetically" and unconvincingly (130). The capacity of the blues to link identities affectively and, moreover, Baldwin's depiction of this dynamic is overlooked by Rosenshield.

8. See Christopher Lane, *The Psychoanalysis of Race,* esp. Slovoj Zizek, "Love Thy Neighbor? No, Thanks!"; Tim Dean, "The Germs of Empires: *Heart of Darkness,* Colonial Trauma, and the Historiography of AIDS"; Julia Reinhard Lupton, "*Ethnos* and Circumcision in the Pauline Tradition: A Psychoanalytic Exegesis"; and Merrill Cole, "Nat Turner's Thing."

9. For a critical study of the forces the Cartesian bifurcation that stand in the way of critical teaching and research, see Joe Kincheloe's "Critical Ontology: Visions of Selfhood and Curriculum" in *Journal of Curriculum Theorizing* (47–64).

10. For a description of this phenomenon, see George Taylor, *The Transportation Revolution, 1815–1860.*

11. For an elaboration of the shifting demographics that gave birth to labor reform and the abolitionist movement, see Eric Forner, *Free Soil, Free Labor, Free Men.*

12. For a more detailed and original account of the paradoxical equation of white racial fragility and dominance, see Julian B. Carter's *The Heart of Whiteness,* 42–74.

13. For modern legal studies on the concept of "property interests in whiteness," see Cheryl L. Harris's "Whiteness as Property."

14. See Robyn Wiegman, *American Anatomies,* 42, for a broader elaboration of how race rose to the status of a "corporeal inscription" along with the privileging of the visual that attends modernity.

15. I borrow liberally here from Matt Brim's "Papas' Baby: Impossible Paternity in 'Going to Meet the Man,'" in which Brim defines Jesse's avoidance of white male impotence as a means of securing and excusing "the white man's own homoerotic internalization of and dependence on his black male counterpart" (185). I use Brim's conception of white male heterosexuality as a social construction linked to the threat of homosexuality and black male sexuality and patriarchy as a way to think more precisely about the ritualized construction of white heteropatriarchy at the intersections of racial and sexual difference.

16. See Roderick A. Ferguson, *Aberrations in Black.* Ferguson addresses the pathologizing of blackness as "nonheteronormative" in African American fiction and canonical sociology, 18, 63. Somerville addresses the same theme in *Queering the Color Line,* focusing on the 1914 film *A Florida Enchantment.*

17. See Sharon Patricia Holland, *Raising the Dead.* Exploring the same theme in *Immigrant Acts,* Lisa Lowe writes: "culture is also a mediation of history, the site through which the past returns and is remembered, however fragmented, imperfect, or disavowed" (x).

Chapter 1. The Melancholy That Is Not Her Own

1. Alberta Hunter's "Downhearted Blues" was adapted and made famous by Bessie Smith in 1923.

2. See Hazel Carby, "Policing the Black Woman's Body in an Urban Context." See also Frank C. Taylor and Gerald Cook, *Alberta Hunter: A Celebration in Blues,* and Ethel Waters, *His Eye Is on the Sparrow.*

3. See Judith Butler, *The Psychic Life of Power,* for an elaboration of how the process of coming to terms with the loss of one's homosexual desire in a society governed by compulsory heterosexuality is a journey of structural mourning always already derailed by melancholia.

4. Stuart Hall explains that we should think of identity as a "'production,' which is never complete, always in process, and always constituted within, not outside, representation . . . and hence . . . able to constitute us as new kinds of subjects, and thereby enable to discover places from which to speak" ("Cultural Identity," 222–37).

5. In *Manliness and Civilization,* Gail Bederman shows how between 1880 and 1917 white men drew on the discourse of civilization to remake white male manliness through and against the image of the primitive and inferior racial Other. In *American Anatomies,* Robyn Wiegman notes the role of performance in securing the ends of this ideological work, suggesting that "We might understand the panoptic and corporeal violence of lynching and castration as a disciplinary practice linked historically to the political and economic reorganizations that accompanied Reconstruction, when

the antebellum figure of the male slave as docile, passive Uncle Tom failed to subdue the anxieties posed by the new conditions attending Emancipation" (13).

6. Bederman's *Manliness and Civilization* outlines a variety of reasons—social, economic, and cultural—Victorian ideologies of manly self-restraint were losing their persuasiveness by the 1880s and 1890s. According to Bederman, G. Stanley Hall, "like many of his contemporaries, began to work to synthesize new representations of the male body which could inform new ideologies of male power" (118).

7. Carter's *Heart of Whiteness* explains this crisis of white ethnic diversity in depth, noting that "In the 1920s and 1930s, when 'normality' was coming to define a mass-cultural sexual standard at least theoretically accessible to all whites, that ideal racial essence retained significant elements of its older composition. In other words, who counted as 'white' changed more, and more quickly, than the contents of the ideal of 'whiteness' itself" (33–34).

8. See Small, *Music of the Common Tongue,* and Erenberg, *Steppin' Out.*

9. Statistic from Williams, "Lynching Records at Tuskegee Institute."

10. Here O'Meally quotes Harry "Sweet" Edison in *Lady Day,* 123.

11. Attali, *Noise: The Political Economy of Music,* is a compelling discussion of this dynamic.

12. For biographical information on Holiday, I relied heavily on O'Meally's brilliantly researched and constructed *Lady Day.*

Chapter 2. Reconstituted Melancholy

1. August Wilson, quoted by David Savran, *In Their Own Words,* 294.

2. Sharon Patricia Holland's analysis in *Raising the Dead: Readings of Death and (Black) Subjectivity* has significantly shaped my understanding here. Holland highlights the unaccomplished nature of American Emancipation, arguing that the enslaved-now-freed person continued to occupy the same space in the country's racial imagination. For Holland, the simultaneous "erasure and presence" of being black in America, of being exploited as a nonentity in the form of slavery's chattel or post-Emancipation America's visible Other, has forced African America to dwell in what she calls a "life-in-death" (17). In her essay, "All the Things You Could Be by Now, If Sigmund Freud's Wife Was Your Mother," Hortense Spillers suggest that W. E. B. DuBois's theory of double consciousness provided a model for locating the experience of "blackness" as an "instance of self-reflexivity" (143).

3. Eng and Han, in "Dialogue on Racial Melancholia," also suggest that racial melancholia presents an important challenge to Freud's contention that melancholia constitutes a pathological disposition that emerges from the disturbances of single-subject psychology. For Eng and Han, the Asian American subject-formation's inability to "get over" and mourn the lost ideal of whiteness is less an individual reality than a social construction.

4. For further discussion of the history of August Wilson's dramaturgy, see Mary Ellen Snodgrass, *August Wilson: A Literary Companion.*

5. I draw on Wilson's *The Piano Lesson* to uncover a paradigm for thinking more

deeply about the social and ritualized determinants and psychical effects of what Roger Luckhurst has called a "transgenerationaly haunted" people (244). Thinking more critically about the notion of haunting as an effect and a dynamic, generative process, I aim to lay bare the role rituals of racialization and racial resistance play in the reconstitution of unresolved racial grief across time and social space on gendered and sexual terms and the consolidation of racialized identities and communities along the way. In doing so, I extend and deepen Nicholas Abraham and Nicholas Rand's metaphysical theory of the phantom by drawing on the psychoanalytic concept of melancholia, the process of racialized subject formation, and ritual to show how reconstituted melancholy secures "the gaps left within us by the secret of the other" ("Notes on the Phantom," 287).

6. In *The Melancholy of Race,* Anne Cheng notes that "Even as we recognize how deeply uncomfortable it is to talk about the ways the racialized minority is as bound to racial melancholia as the dominant subject, we must also see how urgent it is that we start to look at the historical, cultural, and crossracial consequences of racial wounding and to situate these effects as crucial, formulative elements of individual, national, and cultural identities. Only then can we begin to go on to analyze how racialized people as complex psychical beings deal with the objecthood thrust upon them, which to a great extent constitutes how they negotiate sociality and nationality. Within the reductive notion of 'internalization' lies a world of relations that is as much about surviving grief as embodying it" (20). In a similar vein, this chapter is interested in the how melancholy works through ritual to interlock and construct racial identities uniquely in racial community.

7. As Phillip Novak points out in "'Circles and Circles of Sorrow': In the Wake of Morrison's *Sula,*" because "African American culture is still at risk, getting done with grieving might well constitute a surrender to the forces that produced the losses in the first place" (193).

8. In "On Narcissism: An Introduction," Freud defines "sublimation" as a mode of deflection that allows the subject to channel his or her "libidinal" energy in a direction "other than, and remote from" that which is unconscionable (67).

Chapter 3. The Melancholy of Faith

1. In *Gender Trouble: Feminism and the Subversion of Identity,* Judith Butler argues that gender identification is unstable and performative.

2. In "Rethinking the Politics of Race, Gender, and Sexuality," Spurlin explores how *Go Tell It on the Mountain* is "marked by the anxiety and threat of homosexuality under tropes of waywardness, gender dysfunction, and national betrayal in American Cold War discourses of the 1950s, and how these same tropes are redeployed in a new key in the novel's subsequent reception in the Black Power and Black Arts movement in the 1960s, along with *Giovanni's Room* and *Another Country,* where the treatment of same-sex desire is more overt" (59).

3. Indeed, *Go Tell It on the Mountain* was based on Baldwin's personal experience as a young preacher at the Fireside Pentecostal Assembly, where he came to terms with

the role that religion played in filtering his taboo sexual desires through a patriarchal sieve. Baldwin longed for the approval of a stepfather, who eventually served as the constant reminder, in theory and deed, of his illegitimacy. The relationship was Baldwin's most formidable. During the course of their relationship, Baldwin was denied his stepfather's approval and, as a consequence, developed a prepubescent appetite for the affection of other influential men in his life. In fall 1935, Baldwin entered P.S. 24, where he found himself under the guiding influence of Countee Cullen and Bill Porter. These relationships paired with Baldwin's identification with his mother set into motion a mode of compensation for the lack that constituted and mobilized his ego on gendered and sexual terms. These terms Baldwin would not recognize until much later in life. Baldwin's prepubescent journey into what became a homosexual attachment is documented by George Leeming in *James Baldwin: A Biography.*

4. My thinking about deviant masculinity is derived from the work of Kaja Silverman, who, in *Male Subjectivity at the Margins,* "demonstrates that these masculinities represent a tacit challenge not only to conventional male subjectivity, but to the whole of our 'world'—that they call sexual difference into question, and beyond that, 'reality' itself" (1). My thinking about hegemonic masculinity is derived from R.W. Connell's *Masculinities,* in which he defines the concept as "the configuration of gender practice which embodies the currently accepted answer to the problem of the legitimacy of patriarchy, which guarantees (or is taken to guarantee) the dominant position of men and the subordination of women" (76).

5. For more on this undertheorized theme, see Lawless, "The Night I Got the Holy Ghost."

Chapter 4. Queering Celie's Same-Sex Desire

1. Recently there have been several published anthologies exploring the intersections between psychoanalysis and race. See, for example, Abel, Christian, and Moglen, eds., *Female Subjects in Black and White*; Lane, ed., *The Psychoanalysis of Race*; and Eng and Kazanjian, eds., *Loss: The Politics of Mourning.*

2. Alarcón suggests that women of color are hailed by way of many names, racializing, gendering, and sexualizing norms, that are mutually constitutive of one another. For more on this dynamic, see Alarcón's "The Theoretical Subject(s) of *This Bridge Called My Back* and Anglo-American Feminism."

3. Several psychoanalytic scholars have written books or articles that interrogate the relationship between traumatic history and memory. See, for example, LaCapra, *History and Memory after Auschwitz.* For LaCapra, "memory, with respect to trauma, is always secondary since what occurs is not integrated into experience or directly remembered" (21).

4. These included the Inter-Racial Forum of Brooklyn, the Maternal and Child Health Council of West Virginia, and the Mother's Health Association of the District of Columbia.

5. Commenting on this crossing of racialization and deviant sexuality, Wallace notes in *Invisibility Blues* that "In a society in which patriarchal dominance and the

supremacy of the phallus are considered coterminous, the black man is perpetually denied the authority of the Great White Father. The depiction of father-daughter incest in [Toni Morrison's] *The Bluest Eye,* where it completely delimits black family life, focuses intently upon the problem of domestic relations in a community in which patriarchal dominance—as in 'a man's home is his castle'—is always withheld" (232).

6. Statistic from Williams, "The Lynching Records at Tuskegee Institute." James Baldwin's "Going to Meet the Man" (1965) provides a considerably apt paradigm for contemplating how the nexus of lynching and castration tamed the crisis of a fragile racial, sexual, and economic order. Indeed, the threat miscegenation posed to the new, industrial economic order placed much focus on the discourse of race, which ultimately turned attention away from the tension-wrought domain of homosexual desire lodged within the act.

7. In "Gendered Melancholy or General Melancholy?" Hood-Williams and Harrison remind us that "Butler is quite clear that melancholy is not limited to hetero-sexualized gender identities, but works within gay and lesbian identities too" (122).

8. See Butler's *Psychic Life of Power* for a sustained reading of the ambivalent nature of the melancholic subject-formation.

9. See, for example, Wiegman's "Introduction" to *American Anatomies.*

10. David Seelow's *Radical Modernism and Sexuality* nicely explicates how sexuality became a core feature of modernism and the process of modern subject formation. See David Eng's *Racial Castration* for a more extensive discussion of the role of sexuality in racial formation and the place of race in the construction and maintenance of sexual identity.

11. Evelynn Hammonds's "Black (W)holes and the Geometry of Black Female Sexuality" is an in-depth meditation on the relationship between sexual violence and black female subject formation (301–20).

Chapter 5. A Clearing Beyond the Melancholic Haze

1. In *The Melancholy of Race,* Anne Cheng notes that "Dominant white identity in America operates melancholically—as an elaborate identificatory system based on psychical and social consumption-and-denial. This diligent system of melancholic retention appears in different guises. Both racist and white liberal discourses participate in this dynamic, albeit out of different motivations. The racists need to develop elaborate ideologies in order to accommodate their actions with official American ideals, while white liberals need to keep burying their racial other in order to memorialize them" (11).

2. For a brief overview of the harmful effects of naming the harmful effects of racism, see Anne Cheng's *The Melancholy of Race.* For a more detailed explanation of the melancholic ego's inability to grieve its constitutive loss, see Judith Butler's *The Psychic Life of Power.*

3. This chapter rethinks José E. Muñoz's theorization in *Disidentifications* of the productive role of resistance that melancholy plays in the lives of people of color, lesbians, and gays within the broader context of interracial community, exploring

the role theater might play in loosening the psychical grips of the racial melancholy and forging interracial community at once.

4. In *Queering the Color Line,* Siobhan Somerville explores how the discourses of racial and sexual "deviance" were used to reinforce one another's terms about the same time that the 1896 Supreme Court *Plessy v. Ferguson* decision consolidated the racial line and prominent trials began drawing emerging categories of sexual identity. In doing so, Somerville "challenges a persistent critical tendency to treat late-nineteenth-century shifts in the cultural understanding of race and sexuality as separate and unrelated" (3).

5. In *Aberrations in Black,* Roderick Ferguson defines queer of color analysis as an "interroga[tion of] social formations at the intersections of race, gender, sexuality, and class, with particular interest in how those formations correspond with and diverge from nationalist ideals and practices" (149).

6. "Parks evokes this 'posterior,' this history, but the play's Brechtian style suggests that we cannot put it behind us," we are told in Deborah R. Geis's *Suzan-Lori Parks* (79).

7. S.E. Wilmer and others have noted that for Parks, "The stage space is simultaneously historical, contemporary and imaginary" ("Restaging the Nation," 442).

8. In *The Fire Next Time,* James Baldwin notes that "All of us know, whether or not we are able to admit it, that mirrors can only lie" (128).

9. On this point, see Young, "The Re-Objectification and Re-Commodification of Saartjie Baartman in Suzan-Lori Parks's *Venus.*" See also Ben Brently, "Of an Erotic Freak Show and the Lesson Therein." *New York Times,* 3 May 1996, late ed., C3.

10. In "Stranger Than Fiction: The New Multiculturalism and the Case for Psychoanalytic Literary Criticism," I argue that our attempts to harmonize national multiplicity require more critical thinking about the way unconscious meanings and hidden affect condition and cloak the negotiation of racial identity and race relations.

11. For more on conflicting takes on the history of racial and sexual ideology and Baartman, see Zine Magybane, "Which Bodies Matter? Feminism, Poststructuralism, Race, and the Curious Theoretical Odyssey of the 'Hottentot Venus,'" 816–34. He writes: "In the interest of placing Baartman (and racial and sexual alterity) back within history, the remainder of this article will take issue with, and disprove, three of Gilman's core assertions. The first assumption I disprove is that Europeans' fears of the 'unique and observable' physical differences of racial and sexual 'Others;' was the primary impetus for the social construction and synthesis of images of deviance. The second assumption I challenge is that ideas about 'blackness' remained relatively static and unchanged throughout the nineteenth century. The final assumption I critique is that Baartman evoked a uniform ideological response, and her sexual parts represented the 'core image' of the Black woman in the nineteenth century" (817).

12. Eng and Han, for example, argue that the melancholic state is a social interdiction. See "A Dialogue on Racial Melancholia."

13. In "Critical Ontology," Kincheloe states, "One thing our ideological critique of self-production tells us is that the self is a complex, ambiguous, and contradic-

tory entity pushed and pulled by a potpourri of forces. The idea that the self can be reconstructed and empowered without rigorous historical study, linguistic analysis, and an understanding of social construction is a trivialization of the goals of a critical ontology" (58).

14. For an exploration of the nationalist agendas swaddled in racial terms and relations, see Singleton, "Stranger Than Fiction."

15. See Durrant's *Postcolonial Narrative and the Work of Mourning* for a rethinking of Freud's opposition between mourning and melancholia at the level of the collective. Durrant situates the postcolonial project as one of ongoing remembrance. Like Durrant, I too argue for the possibility of freeing the postcolonial era from the effects of historical subjugation and traumas. This chapter, however, perceives this harassment of the dead by the living as an opportunity for productive redirection when experienced in cross-racial community through cultural practice.

Coda

1. In *Toward the African Revolution,* Fanon notes "It is a common saying that man is constantly a challenge to himself, and that were he to claim that he is so no longer he would be denying himself" (3).

BIBLIOGRAPHY

Films

Alberta Hunter: My Castle's Rockin'. 2001. Directed by Stuart Goldman. New York: V.E.I.W. Video.

Cloud Atlas. 2012. Directed by Tom Tykwer, Andy Wachowski, and Lana Wachowski. Los Angeles: Warner Bros.

Dancing: New Worlds, New Forms. 1993. Directed by Rhoda Graur. Long Beach, Calif.: Kutleur International Films.

Lady Sings the Blues. 2005. Directed by Sidney J. Furie. Los Angeles: Warner Bros.

Venus Boyz. 2002. Directed by Gabrielle Baur. New York: First Run Features.

Legal Cases

Plessy v. Ferguson, 163 U.S. 537 (1896).

Published Sources

Abel, Elizabeth, Barbara Christian, and Helene Moglen. Introduction to *Female Subjects in Black and White: Race, Psychoanalysis, and Feminism*. Berkeley: University of California Press, 1997.

Abraham, Nicolas, and Maria Torok. *The Shell and the Kernel: Renewals of Psychoanalysis*. Translated by Nicholas T. Rand. Chicago: University of Chicago Press, 1994.

Abraham, Nicolas, and Nicholas Rand. "Notes on the Phantom: A Complement to Freud's Metapsychology." *Critical Inquiry* 13, no. 2 (1987): 287–92.

Alarcón, Norma. "The Theoretical Subject(s) of *This Bridge Called My Back* and Anglo-American Feminism." In *Making Face, Making Soul: Haciendo*, edited by Gloria Anzaldua, 356–69. San Francisco: Aunt Lute, 1990.

Albertson, Chris. *Bessie*. New York: Stein and Day, 1972.

Alexander, Michelle. *The New Jim Crow: Mass Incarceration in the Age of Colorblindness*. New York: New Press, 2012.

Attali, Jacques. *Noise: The Political Economy of Music*. Minneapolis: University of Minnesota Press, 1985.

Baldwin, James. "Everybody's Protest Novel." In *The Norton Anthology of African American Literature*, edited by Henry Louis Gates and Nellie Y. McKay, 1699–1705. New York: W. W. Norton, 2004.

———. *The Fire Next Time*. New York: Vintage, 1992.

———. "Going to Meet the Man." In *The Norton Anthology of African American Literature*, edited by Henry Louis Gates and Nellie Y. McKay, 1750–61. New York: W. W. Norton, 2004.

———. *Go Tell It on the Mountain*. New York: Knopf, 1953.

———. "Sonny's Blues." In *The Norton Anthology of African American Literature*, edited by Henry Louis Gates and Nellie Y. McKay, 1728–49. New York: W. W. Norton, 2004.

Baraka, Amiri. *Home: Social Essays*. New York: Akashic, 2009.

Barlow, William. *Looking Up at Down: The Emergence of Blues Culture*. Philadelphia: Temple University Press, 1989.

Barrett, Lindon. "'In the Dark': Billie Holiday and Some Sights and Sounds of American Value." *Callaloo: A Journal of African American and African Arts and Letters* 13.4 (1990): 872–85.

Bauman, Zygmunt. *Modernity and Ambivalence*. Ithaca, N.Y.: Cornell University Press, 1991.

Bederman, Gail. *Manliness and Civilization: A Cultural History of Gender and Race in the United States, 1880–1917*. Chicago: University of Chicago Press, 1995.

Benston, Kimberly. *Performing Blackness: Enactments of African American Modernism*. New York: Routledge, 2000.

Bergner, Gwen. *Taboo Subjects: Race, Sex, and Psychoanalysis*. Minneapolis: University of Minnesota Press, 2005.

Boan, Devon. "Call-and-Response: Parallel 'Slave Narrative' in August Wilson's *The Piano Lesson*." *African American Review* 32, no. 2 (1998): 263–71.

Brently, Ben. "Of an Erotic Freak Show and the Lesson Therein." *New York Times*, 3 May 1996, late ed., C3.

Brim, Matt. "Papas' Baby: Impossible Paternity in *Going to Meet the Man*." *Journal of Modern Literature* 30, no. 1 (2006): 173–98.

Brustein, Robert. "On Cultural Power." *New Republic* 216, no. 9 (1997): 31–43.

Butler, Judith P. *Bodies That Matter: On the Discursive Limits of "Sex."* New York: Routledge, 1993.

———. *Gender Trouble: Feminism and the Subversion of Identity*. New York: Routledge, 2006.

———. *The Psychic Life of Power: Theories in Subjection*. Stanford, Calif.: Stanford University Press, 1997.

Carby, Hazel. "Policing the Black Woman's Body in an Urban Context." In *Identities*, edited by Anthony Appiah and Henry Louis Gates, 115–32. Chicago: University of Chicago Press, 1995.

Carter, Julian B. *The Heart of Whiteness: Normal Sexuality and Race in America, 1880–1940*. Durham, N.C.: Duke University Press, 2007.

Caruth, Cathy. *Unclaimed Experience: Trauma, Narrative, and History*. Baltimore, Md.: Johns Hopkins University Press, 1996.

Cheng, Anne Anlin. *The Melancholy of Race: Psychoanalysis, Assimilation, and Hidden Grief*. New York: Oxford University Press, 2001.

Christian, Barbara. "The Race for Theory." In *African American Literary Theory: A Reader,* edited by Winston Napier, 280–89. New York: New York University Press, 2000.

Cohen-Cruz, Jan. *Local Acts: Community-Based Performance in the United States*. New Brunswick, N.J.: Rutgers University Press, 2005.

Cole, Merrill. "Nat Turner's Thing." In *The Psychoanalysis of Race,* edited by Christopher Lane, 261–81. New York: Columbia University Press, 1998.

Connell, R. W. *Masculinities*. Berkeley: University of California Press, 1995.

Davis, Angela Y. *Blues Legacies and Black Feminism: Gertrude "Ma" Rainey, Bessie Smith, and Billie Holiday*. New York: Vintage, 1998.

Dean, Tim. *Beyond Sexuality*. Chicago: University of Chicago Press, 2000.

———. "The Germs of Empires: *Heart of Darkness,* Colonial Trauma, and the Historiography of AIDS." In *The Psychoanalysis of Race,* edited by Christopher Lane, 305–29. New York: Columbia University Press, 1998.

De Lauretis, Teresa. *The Practice of Love: Lesbian Sexual and Perverse Desire*. Bloomington: University of Indiana Press, 1994.

Derrida, Jacques. *Specters of Marx: The State of the Debt, the Work of Mourning, and the New International*. Translated by Peggy Kamuf. New York: Routledge, 1994.

Douglas, Ann. *Terrible Honesty: Mongrel Manhattan in the 1920s*. New York: Noonday Press, 1995.

DuBois, W. E. B. *The Souls of Black Folk*. New York: Penguin, 1989.

Durrant, Sam. *Postcolonial Narrative and the Work of Mourning: J. M. Coetzee, Wilson Harris, and Toni Morrison*. Albany: State University of New York Press, 2004.

Elam, Harry J. Jr. "The Dialectics of August Wilson's *The Piano Lesson.*" *Theatre Journal* 52, no. 3 (2000): 361–79.

———. "Getting the Spirit." In *The Fire This Time: African American Plays for the 21st Century,* edited by Harry J. Elam Jr. and Robert Alexander, xi–xxvi. New York: Theatre Communications Group, 2004.

Elam, Harry J. Jr., and Robert Alexander, eds. *The Fire This Time: African America Plays for the 21st Century*. New York: Theatre Communications Group, 2004.

Ellison, Ralph. "Change the Joke and Slip the Yoke." In *Shadow and Act*. New York: Vintage, 1995, 45–59.

———. "A Party Down at the Square." In *Black on White: Black Writers on What It Means to Be White,* edited by David R. Roediger, 342–49. New York: Schocken, 1998.

Eng, David L. *Racial Castration: Managing Masculinity in Asian America*. Durham, N.C.: Duke University Press, 2001.

Eng, David L., and Shinhee Han. "A Dialogue on Racial Melancholia." In *Loss: The Politics of Mourning*, edited by David Eng and David Kazanjian, 343–71. Berkeley: University of California Press, 2003.

Eng, David L., and David Kazanjian, eds. . *Loss: The Politics of Mourning*. Berkeley: University of California Press, 2003.

Erenberg, Lewis A. *Steppin' Out: New York Nightlife and the Transformation of American Culture*. Chicago: University of Chicago Press, 1984.

———. *Swingin' the Dream: Big Band Jazz and the Rebirth of American Culture*. Chicago: University of Chicago Press, 1998.

Fanon, Frantz. *Black Skin, White Masks*. New York: Grove Press, 1967.

———. *Toward the African Revolution*. Translated by Haakon Chevalier. New York: Grove, 1967.

Ferguson, Roderick A. *Aberrations in Black: Toward a Queer of Color Critique*. Minneapolis: University of Minnesota Press, 2004.

Fisher, James. *The Theater of Tony Kushner: Living Past Hope*. New York: Routledge, 2002.

———. *Understanding Tony Kushner*. Columbia: University of South Carolina Press, 2008.

Fisher, Rudolph. "The Caucasian Storms Harlem." In *The Norton Anthology of African American Literature*, 2nd ed., edited by Henry Louis Gates Jr. and Nellie Y. McKay, 1236–43. New York: W. W. Norton, 2003.

Fitzgerald, F. Scott. *The Great Gatsby*. New York: Collier, 1980.

Flatley, Jonathan. *Affective Mapping: Melancholia and the Politics of Modernism*. Cambridge, Mass.: Harvard University Press, 2008.

Forner, Eric. *Free Soil, Free Labor, Free Men: The Ideology of the Republican Party before the Civil War*. New York: Columbia University Press, 1994.

Forter, Greg. "Against Melancholia: Contemporary Mourning Theory, Fitzgerald's *The Great Gatsby*, and the Politics of Unfinished Grief." *Differences: A Journal of Feminist Cultural Studies* 14, no. 2 (2003): 134–70.

Foucault, Michel. "Repressive Hypothesis." In *The History of Sexuality: An Introduction*, vol. 1. Translated by Robert Hurley. New York: Vintage Books, 1990.

Freud, Sigmund. "The Future of an Illusion." In *The Freud Reader*, edited by Peter Gay, 685–721. New York: Norton, 1989.

———. "Mourning and Melancholia." In *The Standard Edition of the Complete Psychological Works of Sigmund Freud*, edited by James Strachey, 14: 237–58. London, England: Hogarth Press, 1955.

———. "On Narcissism: An Introduction." In *The Standard Edition of the Complete Psychological Works of Sigmund Freud*, edited by James Strachey, 14: 67–102. London, England: Hogarth Press, 1955.

———. "Totem and Taboo: Some Points of Agreement between the Mental Life of Savages and Neurotics." In *The Standard Edition of the Complete Psychological Works of Sigmund Freud*, edited by James Strachey, 13: 1–255. London, England: Hogarth Press, 1955.

Garber, Eric. "A Spectacle in Color: The Lesbian and Gay Subculture of Jazz Age Harlem." In *Hidden from History: Reclaiming the Gay and Lesbian Past*, edited by Martin Baumi Duberman, Martha Vicinus, and George Chauncey Jr., 318–31 New York: NAL, 1989.

Geis, Deborah R. *Suzan-Lori Parks*. Ann Arbor: University of Michigan Press, 2008.

George, Sheldon. "Trauma and the Conservation of African-American Racial Identity." *Journal of Psychoanalysis, Culture and Society* 6, no. 1 (2001): 58–72.

Gilman, Charlotte Perkins. "The Yellow Wallpaper." In *Four Stories by American Women: Rebecca Harding Davis, Charlotte Perkins Gilman, Sarah Orne Jewett, Edith Wharton,* edited by Cynthia Griffin Wolff, 41–58. New York: Penguin, 1990.

Gilroy, Paul. *The Black Atlantic: Modernity and Double Consciousness*. Cambridge, Mass.: Harvard University Press, 1993.

———. *Postcolonial Melancholia*. New York: Columbia University Press, 2005.

Gresham, Jewell Handy. "James Baldwin Comes Home." In *Conversations with James Baldwin,* edited by Fred L. Standley and Louis H. Pratt, 159–67. Jackson: University Press of Mississippi, 1989.

Griffin, Farah Jasmine. *"Who Set You Flowin'?": The African-American Migration Narrative*. New York: Oxford University Press, 1995.

Griffin, Horace L. *Their Own Receive Them Not: African American Lesbians and Gays in Black Churches*. New York: Wipf and Stock, 2010.

Groves, Ernest R. *The Marriage Crisis*. New York: Longmans, Green, 1928.

Hale, Grace Elizabeth. *Making Whiteness: The Culture of Segregation in the South, 1890–1940*. New York: Vintage, 1998.

Hall, Stuart. "Cultural Identity and Diaspora." In *Identity, Community, Culture, Difference*, edited by Jonathan Rutherford, 222–37. New York: Lawrence and Wishart, 2003.

Hammonds, Evelynn. "Black (W)holes and the Geometry of Black Female Sexuality." In *Skin Deep, Spirit Strong: The Black Female Body,* edited by Kimberly Wallace-Sanders, 301–20. Ann Arbor: University of Michigan Press, 2002.

Harris, Cheryl L. "Whiteness as Property." *Black on White: Black Writers on What It Means to Be White,* edited by David R. Roediger, 103–18. New York: Schocken, 1998.

Harris, Trudier. *Black Women in the Fiction of James Baldwin*. Knoxville: University of Tennessee Press, 1985.

———. "From Victimization to Free Enterprise: Alice Walker's *The Color Purple*." *Studies in American Fiction* 14, no. 1 (1986): 1–17.

Harrison, Daphne Duval. *Black Pearls: Blues Queens of the 1920s*. New Brunswick, N.J.: Rutgers University Press, 1988.

Hassoun, Jacques. *The Cruelty of Depression: On Melancholy*. Reading, Mass.: Addison-Wesley, 1997.

Holiday, Billie, with William Dufty. *Lady Sings the Blues*. New York: Broadway Books, 2006.

Holland, Sharon Patricia. *Raising the Dead: Readings of Death and (Black) Subjectivity*. Durham, N.C.: Duke University Press, 2000.

Hood-Williams, John, and Wendy Cealey Harrison. "Gendered Melancholy or General Melancholy? Homosexual Attachments in the Formation of Gender." *New Formations,* issue 41 (Autumn 2000): 109–26.

hooks, bell. *Ain't I a Woman: Black Women and Feminism*. Boston: South End Press, 1981.

———. *Killing Rage*. New York: Macmillan, 1996.

———. *Rock My Soul: Black People and Self-Esteem*. New York: Atria, 2003.

———. *Yearning: Race, Gender, and Cultural Politics*. Boston: South End Press, 1990.

Johnson, Patrick E., and Mae G. Henderson. "Introduction: Queering Black Studies/'Quaring' Black Studies" In *Black Queer Studies: A Critical Anthology*, edited by Patrick E. Johnson and Mae G. Henderson, 1–17. Durham, N.C.: Duke University Press, 2005.

Jones, Leroi. *Blues People: Negro Music in White America*, 2nd ed. New York: Quill, 1999.

Joyce, Joyce A. "'Who the Cap Fit': Unconsciousness and Unconscionableness in the Criticism of Houston A. Baker Jr. and Henry Louis Gates Jr." In *African American Literary Theory: A Reader,* edited by Winston Napier, 319–30. New York: New York University Press, 2000.

Kincheloe, Joe L. "Critical Ontology: Visions of Selfhood and Curriculum." *Journal of Curriculum Theorizing* 19, no. 1 (2003): 47–64.

Krasner, David. "Empathy in Theater." In *Staging Philosophy: Intersections of Theater, Performance, and Philosophy,* edited by David Krasner and David Z. Saltz, 255–77. Ann Arbor: University of Michigan Press, 2006.

Kristeva, Julia. *Black Sun: Depression and Melancholia*. Translated by Leon S. Roudiez. New York: Columbia University Press, 1989.

———. *In the Beginning Was Love: Psychoanalysis and Faith*. Translated by Arthur Goldhammer. New York: Columbia University Press, 1987.

Kushner, Tony. *Caroline, or Change*. New York: Theatre Communications Group, 2004.

LaCapra, Dominick. *History and Memory after Auschwitz*. Ithaca, N.Y.: Cornell University Press, 1998.

Lane, Christopher, ed. *The Psychoanalysis of Race*. New York: Columbia University Press, 1998.

Langer, Susanne K. "Discursive and Presentational Forms." In *Paradigms Regained*, edited by Denis Hlynka and John C. Belland, 415–39. Englewood Cliffs, N.J.: Educational Technology Publications, 1991.

Lawless, Elaine J. "'The Night I Got the Holy Ghost . . .': Holy Ghost Narratives and the Pentecostal Conversion Process." *Western Folklore* 47, no. 1 (1988): 1–20.

Leeming, David. *James Baldwin: A Biography*. New York: Knopf, 1994.

Lott, Eric. *Love and Theft: Blackface Minstrelsy and the American Working Class*. New York: Oxford University Press, 1993.

Lowe, Lisa. *Immigrant Acts: On Asian American Cultural Politics*. Durham, N.C.: Duke University Press, 1996.

Luckhurst, Roger. "'Impossible Mourning' in Toni Morrison's *Beloved* and Michèle Roberts's *Daughters of the House*." *Critique: Studies in Contemporary Fiction* 37, no. 4 (1996): 243–60.

Magybane, Zine. "Which Bodies Matter? Feminism, Postructuralism, Race, and the Curious Theoretical Odyssey of the 'Hottentot Venus.'" *Gender and Society* 15, no. 6 (2001): 816–34.

Marx, Karl. "The Critique of Hegel's Philosophy of Right." In *Karl Marx Early Writings,* edited by T. B. Bottomore. New York: McGraw-Hill, 1963.

McBride, Dwight A. *Why I Hate Abercrombie and Fitch: Essays on Race and Sexuality.* New York: New York University Press, 2005.

McClintock, Anne. *Imperial Leather: Race, Gender, and Sexuality in the Colonial Context.* London, England: Routledge, 1995.

Mercer, Kobena. *Welcome to the Jungle: New Positions in Black Cultural Studies.* New York: Routledge, 1994.

Morrison, Toni. *Beloved.* New York: Plume, 1987.

——. *Playing in the Dark.* Cambridge, Mass.: Harvard University Press, 1993.

Mostern, Kenneth. *Autobiography and Black Identity Politics: Racialization in Twentieth-Century America.* Cambridge, England: Cambridge University Press, 1999.

Muñoz, José Esteban. *Disidentifications: Queers of Color and the Performance of Politics.* Minneapolis: University of Minnesota Press, 1999.

Novak, Phillip. "'Circles and Circles of Sorrow': In the Wake of Morrison's *Sula*." *PMLA: Publications of the Modern Language Association of America* 114, no. 2 (1999): 184–93.

O'Meally, Robert. *Lady Day: The Many Faces of Billie Holiday.* New York: Da Capo Press, 1991.

Parks, Suzan-Lori. *Venus.* New York: Dramatists Play Service, 1996.

Riviere, Joan. "Womanliness as a Masquerade." In *The Inner World and Joan Riviere: Collected Papers, 1920–1958,* edited by Athol Hughes, 90–102. London, England: Karnac Books for the Melanie Lein Trust, 1991.

Roach, Joseph. *Cities of the Dead: Circum-Atlantic Performance.* New York: Columbia University Press, 1996.

Robinson, Randall. *Defending the Spirit: A Black Life in America.* New York: Dutton Press, 1998.

Roediger, David. *Working toward Whiteness: How America's Immigrants Became White.* New York: Basic Books, 2005.

Rosenshield, Gary. "Music and Melancholy: Chekhov's 'Rothschild's Fiddle' and Baldwin's 'Sonny's Blues.'" In *Madness, Melancholy and the Limits of the Self,* edited by Andrew D. Weiner and Lenard V. Kaplan, 122–34. Madison: University of Wisconsin Law School, 1996.

Royster, Philip M. "In Search of Our Fathers' Arms: Alice Walker's Persona of the Alienated Darling." *Black American Literature Forum* 20, no. 4 (1986): 347–70.

Savran, David. *In Their Own Words: Contemporary American Playwrights.* New York: Theatre Communications Group, 1988.

Schocket, Eric. "'Discovering Some New Race': Rebecca Harding Davis's 'Life in the Iron Mills' and the Literary Emergence of Working Class Whiteness." *PMLA: Publications of the Modern Language Association of America* 115, no. 1 (2000): 46–59.

Schor, Naomi. *One Hundred Years of Melancholy*. Oxford, England: Clarendon Press, 1996.

Scott, Daryl Michael. *Contempt and Pity: Social Policy and the Image of the Damaged Black Psyche, 1880–1996*. Chapel Hill: University of North Carolina Press, 1997.

Sedgwick, Eve Kosofsky. *Epistemology of the Closet*. Berkeley: University of California Press, 1990.

Seelow, David. *Radical Modernism and Sexuality*. New York: Palgrave Macmillan, 2005.

Silverman, Kaja. *Male Subjectivity at the Margins*. New York: Routledge, 1992.

Singleton, Jermaine. "Stranger Than Fiction: Whiteness, the New Multiculturalism, and the Case for Psychoanalytic Criticism." *M/MLA: Journal of the Midwest Modern Language Association* 42, no. 2 (Fall 2009): 184–204.

Small, Christopher. *Music of the Common Tongue: Survival and Celebration in African American Music*. London, England: Wesleyan University Press, 1987.

Smith, Anna Deavere. *Fires in the Mirror*. New York: Dramatists Play Service, 1997.

Snodgrass, Mary Ellen. *August Wilson: A Literary Companion*. Jefferson, N.C.: McFarland, 2004.

Somerville, Siobhan B. *Queering the Color Line: Race and the Invention of Homosexuality in American Culture*. Durham, N.C.: Duke University Press, 2000.

Spillers, Hortense J. "'All the Things You Could Be by Now, if Sigmund Freud's Wife Was Your Mother': Psychoanalysis and Race." In *Female Subjects in Black and White: Race, Psychoanalysis, Feminism,* edited by Elizabeth Abel, Barbara Christian, and Helene Moglen, 135–58. Berkeley: University of California Press, 1997.

Spurlin, William J. "Rethinking the Politics of Race, Gender, and Sexuality: The Critical Reception of Baldwin's *Go Tell It on the Mountain* in the Cold War Imaginary and in US Black Nationalism." *MAWA Review* 19, no. 1 (2004): 58–70.

Stringer, Dorothy. *"Not Even Past": Race, Historical Trauma, and Subjectivity in Faulkner, Larsen, and Van Vechten*. New York: Fordham University Press, 2010.

Tate, Claudia. *Psychoanalysis and Black Novels: Desire and the Protocols of Race*. New York: Oxford University Press, 1998.

Taylor, Diana. *The Archive and the Repertoire: Performing Cultural Memory in the Americas*. Durham, N.C.: Duke University Press, 2003.

Taylor, Frank C., and Gerald Cook. *Alberta Hunter: A Celebration in Blues*. New York: McGraw-Hill, 1987.

Taylor, George. *The Transportation Revolution, 1815–1860*. New York: Rinehart, 1957.

Terkel, Studs. "An Interview with James Baldwin." In *Conversations with James Baldwin,* edited by Fred R. Standley and Louis H. Pratt, 3–23. Jackson: University Press of Mississippi, 1989.

Thandeka. *Learning to Be White: Money, Race, and God in America*. New York: Continuum, 1999.

Thompson, Rosemarie G. *Extraordinary Bodies: Figuring Physical Disability in American Culture and Literature*. New York: Columbia University Press, 1997.

Tuhkanen, Mikko. *The American Optic: Psychoanalysis, Critical Race Theory, and Richard Wright*. Albany: State University of New York Press, 2009.

Van Vechten, Carl. *Nigger Heaven*. Urbana: University of Illinois Press, 2000.

Walker, Alice. *The Color Purple*. New York: Pocket Books, 1982.

Wallace, Michele. "The Hottentot Venus." *The Village Voice,* May 21, 1996: 31.

———. *Invisibility Blues: From Pop to Theory*. London, England: Verso, 1990.

Waters, Ethel, with Charles Samuels. *His Eye Is on the Sparrow*. New York: Da Capo Press, 1992.

West, Cornel. "Race and Modernity." *The Cornel West Reader*. New York: Civitas, 1999, 55–86.

Wiegman, Robyn. *American Anatomies: Theorizing Race and Gender*. Durham, N.C.: Duke University Press, 1996.

Williams, Daniel T., comp. "The Lynching Records at Tuskegee Institute." In *Eight Negro Bibliographies*, 1–5. New York: Kraus Reprint, 1970.

Wilmer, S. E. "Restaging the Nation: The Work of Suzan-Lori Parks." *Modern Drama* 43 (2000): 442–52.

Wilson, August. *Joe Turner's Come and Gone*. New York: Plume, 1988.

———. *The Piano Lesson*. New York: Plume, 1990.

Wood, Forrest G. *Black Scare: The Racist Response to Emancipation and Reconstruction*. Berkeley: University of California Press, 1970.

Wright, Michelle M. *Becoming Black: Creating Identity in the African Diaspora*. Durham, N.C.: Duke University Press, 2004.

Zizek, Slavoj. "Eastern Europe's Republic of Gilead." *New Left Review* 183 (1990): 50–62.

———. "Love Thy Neighbor? No, Thanks!" In *The Psychoanalysis of Race*, edited by Christopher Lane, 154–75. New York: Columbia University Press, 1998.

INDEX

Page numbers in *italics* refer to illustrations.

agency in performance, 12–13; performance ghosting, 13; racial visibility/invisibility and, 13

phantasms: Afro-Brazilian Condomblé ritual and, 120; blueswomen as primitive phantasm, 31; history as dialogue of living with dead, 26; Marxist specters in Derrida, 23–24, 54; metaphysics of the phantom, 128–29n5; surveillance of white supremacy, 55; transgenerational haunting in *The Piano Lesson*, 51, 53–58, 60–64, 67, 128–29n5

Piano Lesson, The (Wilson): piano recovery as resistance and compensation, 58–60; plot overview, 52–54; post-Emancipation melancholy in, 8, 23–24, 50–51; transgenerational haunting in, 51, 53–58, 60–64, 67, 128–29n5; unmourned racial injuries in, 57–58, 63

Plato, 105–6

Porter, Bill, 129–30n3

post-Emancipation era: dispersal of melancholia and, 7, 50; lingering racial trauma from slavery and racial subjugation, 120; material compensation and, 59–60; post-Emancipation black body, 14, 16, 19, 128n2; post-*Plessy* raciality of space, 16; Progressive Era belief in psychological risks of Emancipation, 112; racial terror as motive for disavowal, 63, 67, 84–85, 116–17; racial/sexual deviance in, 132n4; repackaged ancestral baggage and, 61–62; scholarly neglect of racial melancholy, 107; ungendering of slave communities and, 58; white male manliness in, 127–28n5. *See also* Great Depression; interwar years

primitivism: Baartman exhibition, 100–101, 104, 107–11, 132n6; discredited sexual repression in blueswomen, 27–28, 31; early twentieth century manhood and, 36; minstrel primitive as reconstruction of Victorian repression, 34–35; racial unassimilability and, 70; sexual deviance and, 94

psychoanalytic theory: African American literary study and, 10; black domestic patriarchy and, 91, 130–31n5; Freudian mourning-melancholia binary, 3–4, 23–24, 115–16, 125n3, 133n15; isolation from social history, 6; jazz/blues sexuality and, 33; multiculture and, 132n10; post-Eman-

cipation racial formations and, 50; queer theory and, 22–23; race/psychoanalysis scholarly literature, 125n2; race-sexuality relationship and, 83–84, 94–95, 123; on religion, 68; sexual deviance problem in, 25; study of mourning/melancholia, 2; sublimation, 62–64

queer theory: generative melancholic agency and, 84–85, 88–93; ironic black male same-sex desire and, 81; psychoanalytic theory and, 22–23, 25; queer of color critique, 86, 132n5; treatment of race in, 84

race/racism: African American self-objectification, 41–42; capitalist circulation of figurations of blackness, 31; categories of social difference and, 29–31; conservative movement response to jazz and, 38–39; creation of whiteness and, 8; Internet racism, 122; multicultural racial policing, 107–8; national psychic instability and, 10–11; *Plessy v. Ferguson* verdict, 16; racial wounding as source of melancholy, 68, 129n6; scientific racism, 8, 24, 33, 100–101; as stand in for gender/sexual anxieties, 36–37; surveillance of white supremacy, 55; visual differentiation and, 104; white slumming, 28, 35, 38–39. *See also* biological race theory; blackness; cross-class white sameness; crossing; racial anxiety; racial identification; racial melancholy; whiteness

race records, 29

racial anxiety: Billie Holiday as racial object, 45–47; lynching and, 17–19; minstrelsy and, 17; national psychic instability and, 10–11; nationalization of black entertainment and, 28–29; sexuality and, 17–19, 23, 123, 127n15

racial identification: antiessentialist identification in artistic works, 105–7; antiessentialist racial identity in *The Piano Lesson*, 51; capitalism and, 5; double consciousness and, 102–3, 128n2; fetishized stereotyped identification, 108–9; foreclosure of identification possibilities, 2–3; national belonging and, 12; psychoanalytic depiction of, 120–21; racial melancholy and, 20–21, 56–57; racialized selfhood in *Caroline, or Change*, 113–14; white melancholic identity, 131n1. *See also* subjectivity

JERMAINE SINGLETON is an associate professor of English at Hamline University.

The University of Illinois Press
is a founding member of the
Association of American University Presses.

_____

University of Illinois Press
1325 South Oak Street
Champaign, IL 61820-6903
www.press.uillinois.edu